Policing Cybercrime and Cyberterror

Policing Cybercrime and Cyberterror

Thomas J. Holt
MICHIGAN STATE UNIVERSITY

George W. Burruss
SOUTHERN ILLINOIS UNIVERSITY CARBONDALE

Adam M. Bossler
GEORGIA SOUTHERN UNIVERSITY

CAROLINA ACADEMIC PRESS
Durham, North Carolina

Copyright © 2015
Carolina Academic Press
All Rights Reserved

Library of Congress Cataloging-in-Publication Data

Holt, Thomas J., 1978-
　Policing cybercrime and cyberterror / Thomas J. Holt, George W. Burruss, and Adam M. Bossler.
　　pages cm
　Includes bibliographical references and index.
　ISBN 978-1-61163-256-9 (alk. paper)
　1. Computer crimes. 2. Cyberterrorism. 3. Police. I. Burruss, George W. II. Bossler, Adam M. III. Title.

HV6773.H653 2015
363.25'968--dc23

2015000194

Carolina Academic Press
700 Kent Street
Durham, NC 27701
Telephone (919) 489-7486
Fax (919) 493-5668
www.cap-press.com

Printed in the United States of America

For my wonderful wife Dr. Karen Holt, and our spectacular daughter Scarlett.
TJH

For my mother, Linda.
GWB

*For my amazing wife Jordan and our two wonderful children,
Kate and Bennett.*
AMB

Contents

Acknowledgments	ix
Chapter 1 • Introduction to Cybercrime and Cyberterror	3
Defining Cybercrime and Cyberterror	6
Cybercrime	6
Cyberterror	9
Situating Local Law Enforcement in the Management of Cyberspace	10
Internet Users	11
Internet Service Providers	12
Corporate Security and Industry	13
Non-Governmental Non-Police Organizations	14
Governmental Non-Police Organizations	14
Public Policing Agencies	15
Local Law Enforcement and Cybercrime Investigation	17
Chapter 2 • Cybercrime Statistics and Officer Perspectives	21
Data Sources for Cybercrime and Cyberterror	22
UCR and NIBRS	22
NCVS	24
IC3	24
Business Estimates	26
Officer Perceptions of Cybercrime	27
Officer Perceptions of Typical Cybercriminals and Victims	28
Perceptions of Cybercrime Uniqueness, Seriousness, and Frequency	29
Assessing Specialized Officers' Perceptions of Cybercrime	34
Summary and Conclusion	38
Chapter 3 • Examining the Attitudes of Local Law Enforcement toward Cybercrime Training	39
Investigative Resources for Cybercrime Cases	40
Officer Interest in Cybercrime Training	43

Officer Attitudes toward Training	48
Summary and Conclusion	58
Chapter 4 • Police Officer Attitudes toward the Law Enforcement Response to Cybercrime	**59**
Perceptions of Traditional Strategies to Combat Cybercrime	60
Support of Cybercrime Investigations within Police Departments	63
Innovative Strategies	66
Interest in Working with High-Tech Industries and Service Providers	71
Summary and Conclusions	88
Chapter 5 • Stress, Strain, and Satisfaction among Cybercrime Investigators	**89**
Job Stress in Policing	90
Occupational Experiences in Law Enforcement	90
Cybercrime, Forensic Investigation, and Stress	91
Assessing Stress, Satisfaction, and Coping Mechanisms	94
Exploring the Predictors of Stress and Satisfaction	98
Coping Mechanisms Reported By Digital Forensic Investigators	103
Exploring Trauma among Digital Forensic Investigators	105
Summary and Conclusions	109
Chapter 6 • Implications for Policing Policy and Practice	**115**
Implications of Findings for CJ Policy	115
1) Public Awareness	115
2) Data Reporting	117
3) Uniform Training and Certification Courses	118
4) Onsite Management Assistance for Electronic Crime Units and Task Forces	119
5) Updated Laws	120
6) Cooperation with the High-Tech Industry	122
7) Special Research and Publications	123
8) Management Awareness and Support	124
9) Investigative and Forensic Tools	126
10) Structuring a Computer Crime Unit	126
Limitations and Conclusions	130
References	**133**
Index	**149**

Acknowledgments

As the field of criminological research on cybercrime continues to evolve, we are grateful to the many individuals whose assistance and contributions facilitated its creation. We are extremely grateful to April Wall-Parker, Deputy Director Mark Gage, Gerry Cliff, and all of the trainers of the National White Collar Crime Center. This study would not have been possible without their creativity and assistance in allowing the researchers to survey trainees in their various courses. We would also like to thank the Charlotte Mecklenburg Police Department and the Savannah Chatham County Metropolitan Police Department for their willingness to allow the researchers to survey line officers in both agencies. They provided us with an opportunity few have had in researching cybercrime; we are greatly appreciative. We would also like to sincerely thank the publishing team at Carolina Academic Press, especially Beth Hall for her encouragement and flexibility throughout the creation and submission of this work. There were times I am sure we tried your patience. It is also important that we thank the faculty and staff of the Department of Criminology and Criminal Justice at the University of Missouri–Saint Louis. Dr. Scott Decker is still a mentor despite our having graduated many years ago. Finally, we would like to thank our families and friends for all of their support throughout this process.

Policing Cybercrime
and
Cyberterror

Chapter 1

Introduction to Cybercrime and Cyberterror

Over the last 30 years, the development of personal computers, cell phones, and the Internet has radically reshaped modern society. The ability to communicate with others in real time via multiple forms of private and public text has simplified the process of interpersonal connectivity. Many of these communications are engendered by cell phones that can also connect to the Internet, providing mobile access to data anywhere. In addition, the World Wide Web has provided a medium for personal expression, entertainment, and consumerism that is unparalleled. Individuals can obtain products and services from around the world and complete financial transactions through various web-based payment systems. Many also use streaming video services like Netflix or Hulu to watch television shows and movies. Print media services are also increasingly adapting their publications to electronic formats and websites to increase readership and promote their products.

The global spread of these technologies now means that people can literally connect to anyone virtually anywhere, enabling cultural synthesis and information sharing that was not otherwise possible. There are now 2.1 billion Internet users around the world, with the largest populations in China and the United States respectively (Central Intelligence Agency, 2011). In addition, the social networking site Facebook has over 1.15 billion user accounts, slightly smaller than the total population of China (Facebook, 2013). Much of these technologies are regularly used by young people, as in the U.S. where 93 percent of individuals under the age of 18 are online (Lenhart & Madden, 2007) and are online for an average of five to seven days a week (Wolak, Mitchell, & Finkelhor, 2006). In fact, there is now a gap between age groups on the basis of whether they were born prior to or after the invention of the Internet (Prensky, 2001).

The benefits afforded by technological innovation are not only evident for behaviors like paying bills and keeping in touch with family and friends, but for deviant and criminal activities as well. Youth regularly use social media and text messaging in order to bully or harass classmates (Hinduja & Patchin, 2009; Jones et al., 2012). Fraudsters leverage global access to victim populations through the distribution of spam emails that suggest the recipient will receive large sums of money with minimal effort (Holt & Graves, 2007; King & Thomas, 2009; Wall, 2004). Sex workers can now identify and arrange meetings with clients via email, text, or the web with no need for street-based interactions (Holt & Blevins, 2007; Sanders, 2008). Pedophiles have begun to use the Internet as a key resource for the exchange of child pornography as well as the solicitation of youth through chat rooms and social networking profiles (Finkelhor, 2008; Wolak, Finkelhor, & Mitchell, 2012).

The development of the Internet has also engendered new forms of offending that could otherwise not exist, such as computer hacking in which individuals attempt to access computer files and data through the Internet (Bachmann, 2010; Holt, 2007; Schell & Dodge, 2002). Attackers can also use malicious software programs to breach sensitive systems and degrade or harm network functionality (Nazario, 2003; Symantec, 2012). Even more disconcerting is the fact that the critical infrastructures that manage and support electricity, sewer, and water utilities are now controlled via Internet-based systems. These resources can be compromised and harmed remotely by nation-states or extremist groups in order to cause widespread harm in the real world (see Brodsky & Radvanovsky, 2011; Rege, 2013).

The evolution of offending behaviors due to the prevalence of technology presents a distinct challenge for citizens, private industry, and most importantly, law enforcement agencies (Brenner, 2008; Goodman, 1997; Hinduja, 2007; Holt et al., 2010; McQuade, 2006; NIJ, 2008; Stambaugh et al., 2001; Taylor et al., 2010; Wall, 2001). For instance, citizens may not know if they can report their experiences to law enforcement. They may be unaware as well that they were even victimized at all. Similarly, businesses and private industry may not report a serious compromise or criminal incident, unless it is legally required, in order to minimize any negative repercussions to their reputation (Brenner, 2011). Private industry also owns or operates the infrastructure that may be used in the course of a technologically enabled offense, such as web servers, Internet connectivity, and cellular services (Andress & Winterfeld, 2011; Brenner, 2008). Thus, these groups have to be willing to meet legal obligations to retain user information that may serve as evidence in the event law enforcement requests access to facilitate an investigation.

As a consequence, law enforcement agencies are somewhat disadvantaged in the investigation of technology-enabled offenses, more commonly referred to as cybercrimes (Wall, 2001). The lack of reporting makes it difficult for officers and agencies to report the scope of victimization or offending in the population they serve. The very nature of computer and cellular telephony allows actors to victimize populations around the world, making it difficult for local agencies to know whether this is an incident they can investigate or if it needs to be pushed up to a state or federal agency. Offenders can also utilize resources such as proxies to conceal their physical location or identity. There are also substantive technological resources required, including forensic analysis software and various hardware, to properly investigate these crimes.

Due to these and other investigative hurdles, our understanding of the process and experience of policing cybercrime is generally limited. The majority of cybercrime investigation in the United States is associated with federal agencies like the Federal Bureau of Investigation (FBI) and the United States Secret Service (USSS) as they have both the resources and mandate to investigate offenses that cross state or national boundaries (Andress & Winterfeld, 2011). These agencies have a much smaller staff and scope to investigate the range of offenses that may occur. As a result, cases that have a limited economic impact or do not affect multiple victims may not be taken on by federal agencies.

The emphasis on federal law enforcement's role in the investigation of cybercrimes and technology-enabled offenses has led to a paucity of knowledge on the role of local police in dealing with these offenses (Stambaugh et al., 2001). A small body of research has considered the perception of cybercrime among administrators or representatives of local agencies (Hinduja, 2004; Holt, Bossler, & Fitzgerald, 2010; Marcum, Higgins, Freiburger & Ricketts, 2010; Stambaugh et al., 2001). A small number have also focused on the perceptions of local line officers toward cybercrimes (Bossler & Holt, 2012; Holt & Bossler, 2012; Senjo, 2004), though there have been few systematic attempts to address the general law enforcement capacity to investigate these offenses from the local to federal level (Stambaugh et al., 2001). Such information is vital to generate policies that can address deficiencies in training, resources, and funding available for law enforcement agencies to appropriately respond to the frequently changing landscape of cybercrimes.

This text is designed to provide an in-depth discussion of the perceptions and responses of law enforcement agencies in dealing with cybercrime and cyberterror. The themes for this book include the challenges that cybercrime and digital evidence handling pose for local and state agencies, the jurisdictional and investigative hurdles that hinder the response capabilities of police agencies, and the complexities of the actual investigation of these offenses and their impact on officers. This text is designed to explore these issues in a non-technical manner to increase the current body of scholarship surrounding policing cybercrime and cyberterror. This text will also compare many forms of cybercrime against traditional offenses in the real world in order to contextualize the response and position of agencies relative to these emerging crime types.

Defining Cybercrime and Cyberterror

Cybercrime

Before discussing the challenges technology-enabled offenses pose to policing, it is necessary to understand the ways that these activities are defined by law. Legislators dictate the law enforcement response to any activity; thus we must understand how and why some crimes are classified at the local and/or federal level. In fact, there is some debate over the appropriate language used to define crimes that utilize technology. The National Institute of Justice, which serves as the research division of the U.S. Department of Justice, developed the term "electronic crime" for use in a seminal study of the capacity of state and local law enforcement to investigate these types of offenses (Stambaugh et al., 2001). In order to capture the complexity and variation in state statutes, "electronic crime" included:

> ... fraud, theft, forgery, child pornography or exploitation, stalking, traditional white-collar crimes, privacy violations, illegal drug transactions, espionage, computer intrusions, or any other offenses that occur in an electronic environment for the purpose of economic gain or with the intent to destroy or otherwise inflict harm on another person or institution (Stambaugh et al., 2001, p. 2).

This definition is legalistic in that it focuses on criminal acts, the motivation of the offender, and the harm resulting from such acts. While this term is certainly helpful for prosecution and in other legal matters, the media and public typically do not use it to discuss these crimes. In addition, it is unclear what exactly is meant or included in the term "electronic environment." Another issue is that including the motivations of the offender, "economic gain or the intent to destroy or otherwise inflict harm," excludes behaviors that are illegal, but are not harmful. For example, many hackers engage in computer intrusion with no intent to commit harm; they simply want to intrude for curiosity and exploration purposes. Thus, using the electronic crimes definition would only include those times when hackers engage in willfully harmful acts. In order to explain hacking behavior, a criminologist would wish to explore the entirety of the hacking subculture, including intrusive but harmless acts as well as intrusive and destructive acts. Therefore, a definition of cyber behavior that is more encompassing of illegal behaviors in cyberspace would be more fruitful.

Instead, two common terms used by most individuals and groups, including researchers, policy makers, law enforcement, information security specialists, and the public, are "cybercrime" and "computer crime." Cybercrimes are those offenses where "the perpetrator uses special knowledge of cyberspace," while computer crimes result when "the perpetrator uses special knowledge about computer technology" (Furnell, 2002, p. 21; Wall, 2001). The distribution of malware, for example, may be viewed as a cybercrime due to the incorporation of the Internet, but the possession of digital images of child pornography may be considered a computer crime. Both of these terms, however, have become synonymous in popular media and academic literature because most all forms of technology can be connected to the Internet through wireless or hard-line Internet connectivity (Furnell, 2002). Thus, cybercrime is the term we will use throughout this text to refer to these offenses.

We use the four-category typology of cybercrime developed by David Wall (2001) as it is both the most well cited and expansive framework used to understand cybercrimes. These sub-dimensions could help differentiate what level of law enforcement should respond and whether they are properly trained and prepared to do so (Wall, 2007). The first category is cyber-trespass, encompassing the crossing of invisible, yet salient, boundaries of ownership online (Wall, 2001). Computer hackers typically engage in cyber-trespass due to their desire to penetrate computer systems that they do not own (Bachmann, 2010; Holt, 2007). Hackers are individuals with a profound interest in computers and technology who have used their knowledge to access computer systems, particularly to engage in malicious or unethical activities (see Holt, 2007; Schell & Dodge, 2002).

Hackers are also responsible for malicious software programs, such as viruses and botnet code, which automate a variety of attacks and break into computer systems (Bacher et al., 2005; Holt, 2013; Symantec, 2013). Malicious programs can disrupt network traffic, capture passwords for sensitive resources, delete or corrupt files, and utilize infected systems for future attacks (Symantec, 2013). For example, U.S. companies who participated in a recent Computer Security Institute survey (2009) reported losing an average of $40,000 dollars per respondent due to viruses and $400,000 due to another form of malware called botnet infections.

The second and related category within Wall's (2001) typology is cyber-deception and theft. This form of computer crime includes all the various criminal acquisitions that may occur online, particularly for thefts due to trespass. In fact, the opportunities to engage in electronic theft have increased significantly with the development and penetration of computer technology and the Internet (see Holt, 2007; Holt & Graves, 2007; Newman & Clarke, 2003; Wall, 2001, 2007). The electronic databases managed by businesses and financial institutions to store sensitive customer information can be accessed and compromised by hackers to quickly and efficiently steal massive amounts of information (Newman & Clarke, 2003; Peretti, 2009; Wall, 2007). In fact, there have been a number of massive data breaches in the United States since 2009 against major retailers and payment processors. Heartland Payment Systems announced in 2009 that a small group of hackers were able to acquire information from 130 million credit and debit cards processed by 100,000 businesses (Verini, 2010). The retailer Target also reported a breach of over 80 million credit cards in 2013, based on a vulnerability in their point-of-sale terminals in the store. Similarly, music and media piracy through computer outlets have caused billions of dollars in losses through lost revenue and jobs (see Business Software Alliance, 2012; Gunter, 2009; Higgins, 2005). For instance, one company estimates that the U.S. recording industry loses over twelve billion dollars each year from piracy (Siwek, 2007).

The third category within Wall's (2001) typology includes cyber-porn and obscenity. Sexually expressive or explicit materials are readily available across the World Wide Web, though they may not be illegal in certain areas. For instance, adult pornography is a multi-million-dollar industry due to the availability of inexpensive recording equipment and high speed Internet connectivity (Edelman, 2009; Lane, 2000). These activities are, however, largely ignored by law enforcement in favor of offenses that are clearly illegal or facilitate criminal activity in the real world. For instance, forums and various websites are now used by both sexual service providers and their customers in order to identify services and solicit encounters (Cunningham & Kendall, 2013; Holt & Blevins, 2007; Milrod & Weitzer, 2012). The Internet has become a popular venue for pedophiles and sexual predators, allowing them to make contact with each other, trade pictures and information, and communicate with potential victims (Durkin, 1997; Jenkins, 2001; McGrath & Casey, 2002; Quayle & Taylor, 2002). In fact, the number of arrests related to child exploitation crimes facilitated by technology has increased dramatically since the year 2000, with over 8,144 arrests occurring in 2009 alone (Wolak et al., 2012).

The final form of crime within Wall's (2001) typology is cyber-violence, representing the distribution of a variety of injurious, hurtful, or dangerous materials online. The first form of cyber-violence includes the use of the Internet as a means to harass others when they are not in the same physical vicinity (Bocij, 2004; Finn, 2004). Harassment can take a variety of forms, such as threatening or sexual messages delivered via e-mail, instant messaging services, or posts in chat rooms (Hinduja & Patchin, 2009). Victims may view harassing communications to be nothing more than a nuisance, though many individuals may feel physical or emotional stress as a consequence (Finkelhor et al., 2000; Finn, 2004). Estimates of online harassment and stalking appear to be on the rise, particularly among young people and college students due in part to frequent Internet use among this population (Bocij, 2004; Finn, 2004; Wolak, Mitchell, & Finkelhor, 2012). A recent national examination of young Internet users found that the rates of online harassment have increased from six percent in 2000 to 11 percent in 2010 (Wolak et al., 2012).

The second form of violence involves the distribution of materials online that can be used to cause harm in the real or virtual world. The distributed nature of the Internet allows individuals to easily distribute bomb-making manuals, guides on guerrilla warfare strategies, and information to facilitate hacking and fraud around the world (Denning, 2011; Wall, 2001). The publication of such information may not pose an immediate risk to any single individual or group, though this information can be used to cause harm by those with sufficient motivation. Additionally, free speech laws in the United States and lax enforcement in various parts of the world may engender the spread of radical positions or ideological documents. In fact, there is some evidence that radical Muslim movements utilize website hosting services in the United States because of the protections afforded to individual civil liberties (Hoffman, 2006).

Cyberterror

The wide range of behaviors that may be classified as cybercrimes create a substantive challenge for law enforcement at all levels. This issue is compounded by the fact that some of these offenses may also be classified as acts of terror depending upon the target and the ideological outlook of the group (see Brenner, 2008). Many nations treat terror incidents as criminal offenses. There are, however, substantive differences between crime and terror regarding motive and the scope of harm caused. For instance, criminal acts often target single individuals and may be motivated by economic or other objectives. Terrorist attacks, on the other hand, are often driven by a political motive and are designed to not only hurt or kill innocents, but to strike fear into the larger population (Brenner, 2008; Britz, 2010; Martin, 2006). There is generally little consensus across governments as to what constitutes an act of physical terror, due to variations in cultural norms, political and religious ideologies, and political relationships (Hoffman, 2006; Martin, 2006; Schmid & Jongman, 2005). The most prevalent elements across all of these definitions recognize terror acts as incidents involving the use of violence for various ideological or political motivations in order to produce fear, intimidate a population, or cause social change in their target (Hoffman, 2006; Schmid & Jongman, 2005)

Similar concepts are present in the range of definitions used to encapsulate acts of cyberterror. This term entered the lexicon in the mid-1990s when computers and the Internet began to play an increasingly significant role in government and industry functions (Britz, 2010; Denning, 2011; Foltz, 2004). Most scholars define cyberterror as the use of digital technology or computer-mediated communications to cause harm and force social change against a civilian population based on ideological or political beliefs (Brenner, 2008; Britz, 2010; Foltz, 2004; Pollitt, 1998). The National Institute of Justice utilized a similarly broad definition of cyberterror in their state and local needs assessment, recognizing any "premeditated, politically motivated attack against information systems, computer programs and data ... to disrupt the political, social, or physical infrastructure of the target" (Stambaugh et al., 2001, p. 2). Thus, physical violence is not necessary in defining cyberterror, as the economic harm or fear produced by a cyberattack against various critical infrastructure may be equivalent to that generated by traditional terror incidents in the real world (see also Denning, 2011; Holt, 2012).

Harm, however, is only one aspect of cyberterror incidents. The communications capability afforded by the Internet and social media allow extremist and hate groups to disseminate their ideas to wide audiences regardless of physical boundaries (Cere, 2003; Gruen, 2005). The ability to widely share marginalized or extreme perspectives ensures that people may be indoctrinated into a social movement and possibly be radicalized toward physical or virtual actions against targets (Gruen, 2005). For instance, the terrorist group Al-Qaeda in the Arabian Peninsula (AQAP) operates an English-language magazine called *Inspire*, which provides information on the perspectives of the group and the jihadist movement generally (Watson, 2013). The glossy magazine format allows the authors to promote their agenda in a way that is both attractive and appealing to readers, including details on simple bomb making to firearm handling techniques. Additionally, the writing style may be engaging and promote the jihadist agenda to those who may never have considered this point of view (Watson, 2013). As a result, the multimedia communications capabilities afforded by the Internet play an important role in the facilitation of terror attacks and extremist movements on- and off-line.

Situating Local Law Enforcement in the Management of Cyberspace

The range of offenses that constitute cybercrime and terror suggest that a sophisticated response is needed to successfully investigate and manage online spaces. In fact, traditional policing agencies are only one facet of the larger response to cybercrimes. Many of the entities involved are not formally charged with the investigation of cybercrimes, though their cooperation is needed in order to successfully investigate these offenses (see Brenner, 2008; Wall, 2007). As a consequence, the role of policing agencies must be situated into the larger network of entities that engage in formal and informal online governance. We will first explore each below and then discuss why local law enforcement agencies are often the least considered, yet perhaps most salient, agencies that should be involved in the investigation of cybercrimes.

Internet Users

The largest proportion of individuals actively engaged in the enforcement of online spaces are the citizens using the Internet every day. People spend a substantial proportion of time online every day each week, primarily in social networking sites like Facebook, Twitter, and Instagram (Lenhart & Madden, 2007). As a consequence end users can serve a vital function in the informal management of behavior since they have the ability to identify unusual behaviors and report it to others shortly after it may appear. This can take the form of reporting harmful or unusual content on social media sites like Facebook and YouTube. Given the tremendous quantity of posts and media put up by users every day, it is nearly impossible for site managers and law enforcement to identify illicit or questionable content on their own. Users are therefore invaluable to help identify such materials and bring it to the attention of others.

Users are also essential to enable reactive policing responses, as they can contact law enforcement agencies in the event that they recognize an illegal activity taking place. Some individuals feel, however, that law enforcement does not take cybercrime seriously or are too busy to investigate every case. As a result, they may take the law into their own hands in order to engage in vigilante activities online. For instance, the website 419eater.com provides a resource for individuals to report scam emails that they receive and reduce their risk of victimization. At the same time, the group provides information on how to engage in "scam baiting," whereby an individual contacts the scammer and leads them on in order to waste their time and resources (419eater.com, 2013). In fact, the group operates a forum for individuals to post their exchanges with scammers, encouraging positive reinforcement for unique scambaiting strategies and outlandish outcomes, like getting photos or scanned passports of scammers.

Other groups operate to aid victims and serve as watchdogs for law enforcement, such as the CyberAngels group, which provides resources for children to stay safe online and avoid sexual solicitations (Wall, 2010). In addition, the group Working to Halt Online Abuse (WHOA) offers resources for advocacy and support of cyberstalking victims. This volunteer organization was created in 1997 in order to aid victims who are experiencing harassment or stalking around the world (WHOA, 2013). WHOA takes reports of cyberstalking incidents from victims who contact the group directly, which they estimate to be between 50 and 75 cases per week (WHOA, 2013). Complaints made by prospective victims are then passed on to their staff of 10 Internet Safety Advocates who work directly with victims around the world in order to determine the source of harassing or stalking messages and contact web hosting services, ISPs and law enforcement (WHOA, 2013).

Internet Service Providers

While Internet users play an important role in the informal identification of illegal activity, the entities that host and provide access to online content have a formal legal obligation to remove harmful content. Specifically, when an individual is interested in creating a website, they must contact an Internet Service Provider (ISPs) to acquire a domain name and access space on a webserver that will host the content on their behalf. The site creator also enters into a legal contract with the service provider where the creator can be held legally liable in the event that they engage in or facilitate illegal behavior. Additionally, ISPs provide Internet connectivity for individuals, which requires that users comply with all applicable local and federal laws. For example, ISPs cooperate with the Recording Industry Association of America (RIAA) to send cease and desist letters to individuals who engage in illegal file sharing of music and movies to deter pirates (Nhan, 2013).

At the same time, ISPs have a legal responsibility to manage the content they host. In fact, the global nature of the Internet means that service providers have to operate within both local and transnational laws. There are no consistent standards regarding the legal liabilities of ISPs (see Brenner, 2011; Wall, 2007), though it is clear that they can be fined in the event they do not comply with regulations set forth by government and industry. As a result, ISPs tend to respond to any request from law enforcement, or individuals in the event of civil litigation to remove hurtful or illicit content (Wall, 2007).

The technical services provided by ISPs can also be invaluable for law enforcement from an evidentiary standpoint as well (Brenner, 2008; Wall, 2007). ISPs maintain data on user activities, such that they can verify that malicious traffic or user activity occurred at a specific location during certain hours. In addition, they may have records of the number of users accessing a website or downloading content from a service they host (Brenner, 2011). Thus, ISPs are a pertinent resource in the formal and informal management of online spaces.

Corporate Security and Industry

The size and scope of law enforcement agencies at both the local and federal level are small relative to the massive size of corporate and industrial security groups, which may be thought of as private police entities. Corporate security personnel are tasked with the protection and management of the assets of their organization, including sensitive information. As a consequence, they play an increasingly pivotal role in the investigation of cybercrime because of the substantive amount of data that they must protect from attacks originating from inside and out of the corporation.

Security officers in corporate settings also sit in a unique position as gatekeepers to law enforcement agencies. Specifically, their primary task is to operate within the best interests of their employer, which may affect when and how they contact law enforcement. For instance, if computer hackers compromise customer accounts at a financial institution, this directly impacts both consumers and the institution's perception in the industry. The number of individual victims affected and the global scope of harm caused may affect the perceived need to make this incident known to law enforcement and individuals outside of the company. The embarrassment, financial harm, or legal liabilities that may arise through public awareness of a break-in can have an impact that equals the harm caused by an attack. As a result, corporate security personnel often work directly with management to determine the need for and timing of any external law enforcement intervention.

In the event that a law enforcement agency is contacted, corporate security serve as the liaison between police and the corporation. Security staff will provide access to all necessary evidence and aid in the identification of staff that may have information about the incident in order to facilitate law enforcement investigations. This role is critical in order to minimize any loss of productivity or strain on computing resources within the company due to the seizure of equipment or records. Thus, security personnel can serve to insulate management and employees from the investigative process while at the same time facilitate the mission of law enforcement agencies.

Non-Governmental Non-Police Organizations

Due to the variety of cybercrimes that may occur relative to the size and capacities of law enforcement, a number of groups working outside of law enforcement and government have emerged to aid in the investigation and response to cybercrime. These groups are often referred to as Non-Governmental Organizations (NGOs) due to the fact that they may operate in concert with government agencies but have no formal responsibility to enforce laws (Wall, 2007). As such, they are informal management and regulatory groups that may serve more as gatekeepers for information or reporting. These groups are also able to operate more quickly and efficiently due to the fact that they do not operate within a bureaucratic structure that can often limit the response capabilities of traditional law enforcement and regulatory agencies (Wall, 2007). For instance, Computer Emergency Response Teams (CERTs) operate around the world to provide coordinated response and investigative capabilities for incidents of hacking and malware attacks (Andress & Winterfeld, 2011). This includes the publication of information concerning vulnerabilities in well known software and hardware, as well as providing malware analysis and forensic capabilities in the event of an intrusion (Holt, 2003).

Governmental Non-Police Organizations

While most all of the groups described thus far play a primarily informal role in the management of online spaces, formal regulatory roles are primarily reserved for governmental agencies and those with a legislative mandate to investigate or prevent cybercrimes (Wall, 2007). There are a range of agencies within the United States that have a role in the prevention and investigation of offenses, though they do not have the capacity to arrest or otherwise sanction offenders. For instance, the U.S. Department of Energy (DOE) plays a critical role in the maintenance and protection of energy programs and production generally. As our energy infrastructure is becoming dependent on the Internet and computer technology for operation and management, the threat of external attacks and compromise have increased dramatically (Department of Energy, 2013). Thus, the DOE operates the Office of Intelligence and Counterintelligence in order to generate intelligence on various threats to our energy infrastructure, as well as those of foreign governments and nations. In addition, the Office of the Chief Information Officer at DOE supports various resources to communicate information on cybersecurity threats to national security generally (Department of Energy, 2013). They support computer security protocols for DOE employees and techniques to secure various resources from external threats.

In addition to the DOD, the National Security Agency (NSA) plays a critical role in the protection and investigation of attacks against sensitive military networks (NSA, 2013). The NSA serves as a key resource in both data encryption and protection of nearly all federal government computer networks. They also investigate attacks against computer networks from nation-state and non-nation state actors alike (NSA, 2013). Finally, they play a critical role in intelligence gathering of foreign nations' cyber-infrastructure in order to map vulnerabilities and develop offensive cyber-strategies. The NSA combines agents with skills in computer science, engineering, mathematics, and linguistics in order to better investigate various issues related to cybersecurity threats.

Public Policing Agencies

The final entity involved in the formal regulation of online spaces are publicly funded policing agencies that have the power and mandate to arrest and enforce laws at the local and federal level (see also Brenner, 2008; Wall, 2007). These groups are by the far the smallest entities engaging in the enforcement of law, though they are the most immediately recognizable resource by citizens due to their role in real world place management. In the United States, policing agencies are structured around diverse and decentralized forces separated by federal, state, and municipal forces. Federal agencies such as the Federal Bureau of Investigation and the U.S. Secret Service often receive the greatest focus by researchers because of their ability to investigate offenses where the offender crosses state or international boundaries in order to access their victim (Brenner, 2008; Wall, 2007). In fact, the FBI is mandated to investigate cybercrimes that target financial institutions, attacks against government and industry resources, and offenses that target children, such as sexual solicitation and the distribution of child pornography.

While large scale cybercrimes perpetrated by foreign entities or that which affect hundreds of victims may draw media attention, they may comprise a small proportion of all cybercrimes that occur. For instance, local agencies are increasingly investigating and arresting offenders involved in the trade or consumption of child pornography (Jones et al., 2013). Similarly, arrests for sexual solicitation and prostitution cases involving technology have increased among local police agencies (Cunningham & Kendall, 2013). These cases have a much more immediate likelihood of involving a local victim and offender and may be successfully investigated using existing investigative resources and strategies.

Regardless of whether the incident is local or international in scope, cybercrime victims may first reach out to local law enforcement to report the incident because they may believe they have the investigative responsibility. Several scholars argue that local patrol officers can be effective first responders to cybercrimes because of their proven success in real world criminal investigations (Brenner, 2008; Goodman, 1997; Hinduja, 2007; McQuade, 2006; Stambaugh et al., 2001; Wall, 2007). Recent government training manuals have been developed specifically toward local officers to improve their understanding of and capacity to properly handle cybercrime investigations starting with basic evidence handling in real world scenes (NIJ, 2008; Stambaugh et al., 2001). In fact, NIJ's (2008) "Electronic Crime Scene Investigations: A Guide for First Responders" is tailored toward patrol officers detailing the steps that responders need to take when arriving at a crime scene that may involve digital evidence, including how to recognize, seize, document, handle, package, and transport evidence from the scene.

Thus, it is imperative that researchers begin to consider the attitudes and perceptions that local officers have toward cybercrimes and assess their ability to respond to these offenses. There is, however, a substantial degree of variation in the size and response capabilities of local law enforcement. In fact, there are roughly 18,000 separate law enforcement agencies in the United States at the local, state, and federal level. The majority of law enforcement agencies serve small populations in rural or suburban communities with populations under 50,000. The jurisdiction and response capability of each agency varies based on their location within this hierarchy. In addition, these agencies have a need to cooperate in order to investigate and manage catastrophic incidents and acts of terror, which may affect large populations.

Municipal agencies also have the greatest disparity in personnel, with agencies that may range from one or two employees up to the New York City police department, which has approximately 36,000 sworn officers. As of 2008, about half of all local agencies had less than 10 sworn officers, and 75% of these agencies served less than 10,000 total citizens (LEMAS, 2010). As a result, most agencies at the local level are focused on three functions: law enforcement, order maintenance, and community service. In addition, many officers in small municipal agencies are generalists, in that they do not have specialized training or a distinct role within the office. While an officer may have a distinct title or rank such as detective or sergeant, they may still have to serve traffic duty and respond to calls for service. Thus, the municipal law enforcement agency has a greater variation in response capability and overall investigative resources based on the tax base and population size they service.

At the next level of organization lie county law enforcement, or sheriff offices or departments, who are responsible for policing those areas outside of municipal boundaries. These offices have a much larger territory than a city police department and vary based on the population of the county served. In addition, sheriff's offices are usually headed by either an appointed or elected officer. As of 2008, there were 2,063 offices with at least one full-time officer and approximately 60 percent of these agencies had fewer than 25 sworn officers (LEMAS, 2010). Sheriff's offices in larger counties serve multiple duties outside of law enforcement and order management. Specifically, they often facilitate traditional county needs such as tax collection, court and jail functions, public building oversight, and in some cases management of coroner services.

State police agencies are the next level of law enforcement, which serve primarily as highway traffic control and management. These agencies may also respond to rural and suburban crime management needs when sheriffs or city police agencies are unable to respond due to jurisdictional conflict or limited resources. State police agencies also increasingly provide forensic laboratory needs for state and local agencies and manage repositories of data through fusion centers to develop crime and terror intelligence. Thus, they are a key resource that serves to augment, rather than supplant local agencies.

Local Law Enforcement and Cybercrime Investigation

In light of the range of offenses that can be defined as cybercrime and the complex relationships between the entities involved in the investigation and response to these offenses, it is vital that researchers investigate how these agencies are adapting and responding to cybercrime calls for service. More than a decade ago, the National Institute of Justice funded a study to identify the strengths and weaknesses of state and local law enforcement agencies' responses to cybercrime. The findings indicated that there were limited investigative resources, personnel, and training available to these agencies. They made ten recommendations to improve the capability of local and state law enforcement agencies (Stambaugh et al., 2001; pp. 2–3). These ten areas included:

1) Public awareness: the public and private sectors need to be better educated on the growing threat of computer crimes to decrease the likelihood of victimization;

2) Data and reporting: Statistics and data collection on computer crime are needed to better understand the prevalence and incidence of computer crime, and to develop trends based on these offenses;

3) Uniform training and certification courses: Justice system actors, including prosecutors and judges, need better training and certifications to effectively deal with computer crimes at all levels of the system;

4) Onsite management assistance for electronic crime units and task forces: State and local law enforcement agencies must develop computer crime units, as well as collaborative task forces to better investigate computer crime cases;

5) Updated laws: Continuously updated legislation against computer crimes is needed to effectively prosecute cutting edge criminal acts and those crimes that cross jurisdictional boundaries;

6) Cooperation with the high-tech industry: The need for greater collaboration and communication with private industry is needed to increase reports of criminal incidents and improve high-tech crime training for law enforcement;

7) Special research and publications: A guidebook with information on training and investigative resources is needed to improve communications between investigators, forensic experts, management, and practitioners to deal with computer crime;

8) Management awareness and support: Law enforcement management and administrators must recognize the severity of computer crime and better support the investigation of these offenses;

9) Investigative and forensic tools: Better technological resources are needed to improve the investigation of computer crime cases, including budget conscious equipment to engender forensic examinations; and

10) Structuring a computer crime unit: Research is needed to explore the needs and staffing issues present in the development of computer crime and forensic investigation units to create a best practices guide for law enforcement agencies.

In the years since the report was published, there have been no real systematic attempts to consider the ways these recommendations have been integrated into the mission of local law enforcement. Furthermore, the criminal justice research community has only begun to assess the ways that local agencies view cybercrimes and their impact on the communities they serve.

In this book, we will consider these issues in the context of local and state agencies using a range of quantitative data sets collected from across the U.S. Each chapter will have a distinct focus on aspects of the state and local law enforcement response.

In Chapter 2, we examine the resources and abilities of local police and law enforcement officers, especially those on patrol. The chapter focuses on: (1) the scope of reporting of cybercrime; and (2) the perceived value of cybercrime investigation among local agencies and cybercrime investigators using various data sets. In particular, the findings will explore how line officers value cybercrime cases relative to real world offenses based on severity of offense and victim impact. This chapter will also consider officer perceptions of cybercriminals in domestic and foreign contexts.

Chapter 3 explores officers' abilities to act as first responders for a variety of cybercrime and cyberterror types. This chapter considers the use of specialized cybercrime units and their growth using Law Enforcement Management and Administrative Statistics (LEMAS) data to track the growth of resources dedicated to cybercrime investigation based on organizational data, such as size, region, and perception of the cybercrime problem between 2000 and 2007. This chapter also examines officer attitudes toward computer training using data from two cities to understand what officers may be more appropriately suited to improved training and resources.

Chapter 4 expands from the previous chapters to assess how officers perceive the value of various strategies to combat cybercrime within the community and across private industry. The chapter considers officer perceptions of the ways that cybercrime cases are supported within their agencies. This analysis is followed by an exploration of the factors associated with officer support for working with the community through community-oriented policing style programs using data from police officers in two cities.

Chapter 5 considers the realities and challenges cybercrime investigators face in the course of their jobs using quantitative and qualitative data. Specifically, this chapter explores the levels of occupational stress among officers who engage in online investigations and the analysis of digital evidence, as well as their levels of job satisfaction. The coping strategies employed by examiners are also examined to consider the physical and emotional impact of work tasks on examiners, as well as the prevalence of secondary trauma and intrusive thoughts. The use of counseling services and other mental health resources by cybercrime investigators will also be considered.

Chapter 6 concludes this work with a synopsis of the larger issues raised throughout the text and discuss various policy initiatives that may improve the overall law enforcement response to cybercrime. The final chapter discusses the various technological and policy changes needed to increase the investigative response of police agencies, as well as detail various internal policies to improve support for investigators. Additionally, the chapter provides a discussion on future trends in law enforcement roles in cybercrime and cyberterror at the local, state, and federal level.

Chapter 2

Cybercrime Statistics and Officer Perspectives

Victims of crime will call the police for serious criminal acts or in incidents in which the victim believes the police can and will help. Most of these calls are to local law enforcement agencies because of the perception that they are the appropriate agency to contact. For example, most burglaries go unsolved (about 88 percent in 2010 according to the FBI), yet most victims will call the police because they feel the burglars have violated their homes' security. Victims do not, however, report cybercrimes to the police because either they assume the police cannot assist them or that the police will not believe their claim. For instance, it is thought that victims of email-based frauds do not contact police because of embarrassment over responding to what are otherwise obvious scams (e.g., King & Thomas, 2009). Research on victims of cyberstalking found that many do not contact police because they think that it will not be taken seriously, or that it may actually exacerbate their experience (Nobles, Reyns, Fox & Fisher, 2012). In addition, since cybercriminals operate in virtual environments with near invisibility, some victims may not recognize the crime until the criminals use the stolen information or some other evidence demonstrates criminal activity has occurred.

These conditions have led to a substantial "dark figure of cybercrime," meaning we do not know the scope of the problem of various forms of offending or the rate of victimization. Though there are various data sources that can be used to understand the number of real world crimes known to police, or reported by victims, such resources are largely unavailable for cybercrimes. As a consequence, individuals who recognize they have become victims of cybercrime may feel lost and unable to contact anyone for assistance. They may even partially responsible for their experience (e.g., Furnell, 2002; Holt, 2003). Citizens' reactions to cybercrime also influence officers' perspectives because the lack of calls for service may foster the belief that it is not a problem, or it is not something the police should investigate.

In order to understand the state of cybercrime reporting, and its prospective relationship to line officers' perceptions of these offenses, this chapter will explore both of these issues in detail. First, we will survey the available resources for crime reporting in the U.S. for the presence or absence of information on cybercrime. We will then examine the existing literature regarding police perceptions of the prevalence of cybercrime and offenders involved in these incidents. The chapter concludes with an assessment of a sample of local line officers' views on the severity of cybercrimes and the frequency with which they occur.

Data Sources for Cybercrime and Cyberterror

The law enforcement response to cybercrime often depends on how the police define the problem and whether they consider the offense serious enough to merit a response. Such police procedural definitions would include not only whether they consider the offense to be property- or violence-related, but also the amount and extent of harm (see Brenner, 2008; Furnell, 2002; Wall, 2001). For example, a victim who purchases a cheap item from an online auction site only to find the seller misrepresented its value will likely not lead to a police investigation (Internet Crime Complaint Center, 2010). On the other hand, someone who is stalked and threatened through the Internet is likely to garner police attention because of the potential for injury or harm to an individual (Catalano, 2012).

UCR and NIBRS

When an individual decides to contact police for assistance and a report is generated by the officer, this complaint is ideally logged and maintained as a statistic to demonstrate how many crimes were made known to a police agency (FBI, 2004). The Uniform Crime Report, the primary resource for police statistics in the United States, provides detailed statistics on both crimes reported to the police as well as incidents cleared, or solved by arrest, as provided by local law enforcement across the country. Over 90 percent of all agencies provide their statistics to the FBI, who in turn aggregate these reports into the UCR to develop information on the crime problem in the U.S. The UCR provides information on all serious felony offenses, or Part I crimes, including homicides, aggravated assaults, robbery, forcible rape, burglary, larceny-theft, motor vehicle theft, and arson. Additional statistics are collected on a range of less serious felonies and misdemeanor offenses, including simple assaults, fraud, vandalism, and prostitution.

Though the UCR provides a robust set of statistics regarding street crimes, they do not include any way to disaggregate cybercrimes or offenses that may have been facilitated by computers and the Internet. The FBI has taken the position that if such offenses were to be included in a new category of cybercrime, it would otherwise distort the historical depiction of crime trends in the U.S. (FBI, 2000). Specifically, separating forms of fraud as physical or cyber-based would make it difficult to understand how or why crime rates may subsequently change.

In order to improve this reporting problem, the National Incident Based Reporting System (NIBRS) was developed by the FBI in 2001 to collect as much information about crimes as possible, including over 40 offense types. Unlike the UCR, NIBRS allows detailed information about every incident of crime reported to police to be recorded and aggregated. Such refinement is not possible in the UCR based on its reporting rules and requirements, thus NIBRS data should provide a more comprehensive set of information regarding crime.

In particular, the offense list within NIBRS includes a category specifying whether the police suspect the offender: (1) used a computer in the commission of a crime; or (2) whether the computer was the object of the crime (FBI, 2000). This information could ideally provide an initial estimation for the scope of cybercrimes reported to law enforcement.

NIBRS' value in assessing the state of cybercrime has not, however, translated into consistent or sound estimates of cybercrime offending. To date, few studies have attempted to estimate the prevalence of cybercrime using NIBRS data due to the limited number of agencies reporting to NIBRS and the difficulty in separating cybercrimes from real world offenses (e.g., Finkelhor & Ornrod, 2004). Part of this challenge stems from the fact that every law enforcement agency that reports to NIBRS has the ability to determine how they will classify an incident. There are guidelines provided that specify how incidents should be coded, but there is no guarantee each agency will follow these suggestions (FBI, 2000). In addition, the single identifier that a computer was used in the course of an offense does not necessarily guarantee that the incident is a cybercrime.

At present, the only forms of cybercrime that can be readily derived from NIBRS data are sexual offenses against children and various forms of fraud. For those instances where a computer was involved, there is the potential to capture the prevalence of these crimes (Finkelhor & Ornrod, 2004). The errors otherwise present make it difficult to disaggregate these crime types from traditional offenses. Furthermore, the current reporting rate for NIBRS is approximately 25 percent of the total United States (FBI, 2014). Thus, the data are extremely unreliable as an estimate for the total incidence of any form of cybercrime in general. In fact, recent research has surveyed law enforcement agencies regarding their arrests for child sexual exploitation crimes in order to create better estimates rather than depending on official statistics (Mitchell & Jones, 2013).

NCVS

Similar issues are evident in the other primary data sources regarding victimization in the United States. The National Crime Victimization Survey (NCVS), which collects data from nationally representative samples of the population to assess victimization and reporting, has not added cybercrime victimization to its main survey instrument. The NCVS has developed small supplemental studies to capture data on cyberstalking (Catalano, 2012) and identity theft (Baum, 2004; Langton, 2011), though measures are not consistent over time. For instance, the NCVS-Supplemental Survey (NCVS-SS) (Catalano, 2012) used a population of 65,270 people collected in 2008 to assess the rate of cyberstalking. The survey found that 26.1 percent of those who reported being stalked received emails that made them fearful (Catalano, 2012). These measures, however, are prone to error and must be carefully considered. In 2012, the Bureau of Justice Statistics revised the NCVS-SS to exclude incidents of repetitive and unsolicited communications, which were spam messages incorrectly classified as either harassment or stalking. This correction did not dramatically decrease the rate of cyberstalking, though it demonstrates the challenges evident in measuring cybercrimes (Catalano, 2012).

IC3

Given a lack of data from official sources, one of the few resources used to measure cybercrime comes from the Internet Crime Complaint Center (IC3). Like the UCR, the IC3's data depends on victims reporting crimes to the police. Established in 2000, the IC3 is located in Fairmont, West Virginia. Its creation was a joint effort by three federal agencies: the FBI, the National White Collar Crime Center (NW3C), and the Bureau of Justice Assistance. The NW3C is a federally funded training and research organization; its principal mission is to sponsor computer training for law enforcement agencies (NW3C, 2014). In addition, the NW3C sponsors the White-Collar Crime Research Consortium, an academic organization with members who research white-collar crime (NW3C, 2014). The Bureau of Justice Assistance is a federal agency supporting law enforcement policies and programs through funding grants (NW3C, 2014). The IC3 is staffed with FBI agents, analysts, and technical support staff as well as supervisors and information technology specialists from the NW3C.

The IC3 receives victim complaints from the public on crimes committed through the Internet. Victims contact the IC3 through an online complaint form that collects information about the victim, the offenders (if known), and the offense. The IC3 staff then analyzes this information. The IC3 staff reports details on the age and sex of the victim and offender as well as the location of the offense victimization or commission. When appropriate, the IC3 staff refers criminal complaints to the appropriate local, state, or federal agency (NW3C, 2014). In addition to acting as a referral service for citizens, the IC3 provides timely information about specific Internet crimes and trends to law enforcement agencies. The IC3 can also estimate trends in Internet crime for specific jurisdictions to aid in their knowledge of local problems. In addition to collecting information from the public, the IC3 publishes Internet crime reports and public service announcements. In sum, the IC3 acts a reporting hub for victims of Internet crime as well as a resource for law enforcement agencies.

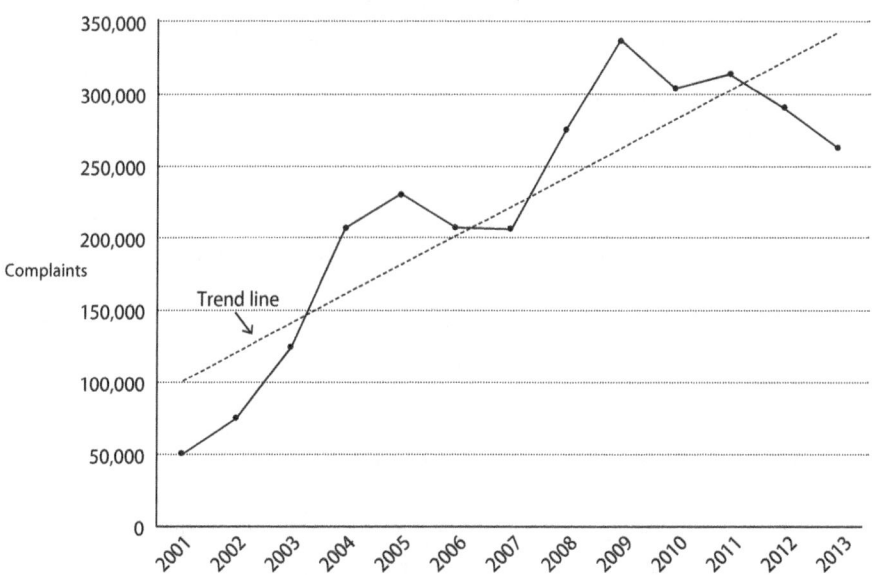

Figure 2.1: Trend in Complaints Reported to the IC3

Note: The solid line indicates the trend in reported complaints; the dotted line is the interpolated linear trend. *Source:* Internet Crime Complaint Center (2014).

The data reported to the IC3 indicates that the trend in Internet complaints is increasing. Figure 2.1 shows the annual number of reported complaints from May 2000, when the IC3 began accepting complaints, to the end of 2011, the latest available data. Note that the slope is positive and fairly steep, indicating the number of complaints has been steadily increasing from 16,838 in 2000 to 262,831 in 2013. Like all official report of data, care must be taken when considering this particular finding. In the case of the IC3, the growth in reporting could result from the success of promoting the center and its website rather than an actual increase in cybercrime reporting generally.

The top five reported crime types in 2013 according to the IC3 comprise about 15 percent of all complaints (IC3, 2014). The most common scheme was auto auction where someone lists a vehicle they do not own, often claiming a job relocation requires a quick, discounted sale (5 percent of complaints). The second most common scheme involved real estate sale (4 percent). These schemes are similar to fraudulent auto sales in that the victim is asked for a down payment for property at greatly reduced prices; the offender then keeps the initial payment but the property is fictitious. Next are FBI scams in which someone posed as an FBI employee in an attempt to defraud the victim by gathering identifying information—social security or bank account numbers (4 percent). The fourth most common was romance scam theft at less than 1 percent, followed by ransomware/scareware scams—victims are intimidated into paying money for decrypting their computer after a virus locks them out (at about 1 percent). Note that most of these fraudulent scams results in identity theft of one kind or another.

The IC3 also reported the demographics and geographic distribution of complaints. The IC3 (2014) reported that the distribution of complainants by sex of the victim was roughly equal between males and females (52.27 percent male), which was typical of the past few years. As for the age distribution, those aged 40–59 filed the most complaints (42 percent), followed by those 20–39 (39 percent), then those 60 or older (15 percent), and finally those 20 and under (3 percent). As for geography, the top ten states in complaints by percentage of total was California (12 percent), Florida (7 percent), Texas (7 percent), New York (5 percent), Pennsylvania (3 percent), New Jersey (3 percent), Illinois (3 percent), Virginia (3 percent), Ohio (3 percent), and Georgia (3 percent). Furthermore, in 2013, the total reported losses were $781,841,611 with an average overall amount lost of $2,975 from total complaints reported.

Business Estimates

The Bureau of Justice Statistics, along with other federal agency partners, reported on a survey of U.S. businesses about experience with cybercrime in 2005 (Bureau of Justice Statistics, 2008). This business victimization survey was a national representative sample from the population of over seven million U.S. businesses. Of the 35,596 companies surveyed, a little over 8,000 responded for a response rate of 23 percent. The survey results reported cybercrime incidents (i.e., attacks and theft) on several different structural dimensions: industry, business size, and risk level (e.g., critical infrastructure, high risk, moderate risk, and low risk).

Overall the results showed that two-thirds of the companies reported at least one cybercrime incident. Fifty-eight percent of companies reported a cyber attack, 11 percent reported cyber theft, and 24 percent reported some other kind of computer security incident. The industries of telecommunications, computer systems design, and durable goods manufacturing reported the highest rates of computer crime incidents at 82 percent, 79 percent, and 75 percent respectively. Overall, the companies in the survey reported losses of $867 million in 2005, both from cyber theft and attack. In addition, businesses reported over 323,900 hours of system downtime.

The survey results indicate that companies experience many cybercrime incidents; however, most companies did not report these incidents to law enforcement. Eighty-seven percent of the companies reported an incident to some entity, but only 15 percent of those businesses reported to law enforcement (local, state, or federal). Most of those incidents reported to law enforcement were about cyber theft (56 percent). The reasons for not reporting varied, but similar to other white-collar crime victims: nothing to be gained (50 percent); did not think to report (22 percent); did not know who to contact (11 percent); outside of law enforcement's jurisdiction (7 percent); adverse publicity or decreased confidence would result (3 percent); and other reasons (11 percent).

Officer Perceptions of Cybercrime

Given the general lack of strong statistical evidence on the prevalence of cybercrime, it is necessary to ask what police think about these crimes. Do they think cybercrime is a prevalent or rare problem based on the small number of incidents reported to their agencies? A limited body of scholarship has examined how local police perceive various forms of cybercrime. These studies analyze survey data or interview transcripts of police department administrators or representatives rather than line officers who interact with the public (Hinduja, 2004; Marcum et al., 2010; Stambaugh et al., 2001). This small body of research indicates local law enforcement agencies do not place a high priority on computer crimes (Hinduja, 2004; Stambaugh et al., 2001). There is one exception: child pornography or child-exploitation crimes. Additionally, law enforcement appears to have increased its focus on financial crimes, such as online fraud and identity theft, but it has placed minimal emphasis on hacking and computer intrusion cases (Holt et al., 2010; Stambaugh et al., 2001). Beyond child pornography and finance-based offenses, police agencies may view cybercrimes as a distraction from more traditional offenses, such as homicide and drug crimes (Hinduja, 2004; Holt et al., 2010).

Patrol officers have largely been excluded from research, even though they are the individuals most likely to respond to calls for service involving cybercrimes at the local level. The reason for this methodological oversight is not clear because patrol officers are commonly surveyed for studies on community-oriented policing, occupational stress, and other criminal justice issues (e.g., Alpert et al., 2006; Haarr & Morash, 1999; Lord, 1996; Morash, Haarr, & Kwak, 2006). Consequently, details are lacking on how officers view cybercrimes or their thoughts on the frequency of these offenses. Examining these issues from the officer level will also serve as a point of comparison to administrator survey responses.

Officer Perceptions of Typical Cybercriminals and Victims

The research on police officers demonstrates that their opinions vary about the typical cyber criminal's demographic characteristics (e.g., Senjo, 2004; Holt et al., 2010). Studies from the early 2000s indicate that law enforcement viewed cybercriminals as older individuals (Furnell, 2002; Senjo, 2004). This may be a consequence of the relatively novel nature of the Internet at the time and the lack of knowledge among the general public as to who engaged in cybercrime (Furnell, 2002). Recent research by Bossler and Holt (2012) found that only 27 percent of officers from Savannah and Charlotte believed individuals committed the majority of cybercrimes in their teens and twenties. In Holt et al.'s (2010) analysis of attendees receiving cybercrime training at FLETC, however, almost half (48.5 percent) of the trainees believed that the majority of offenders were younger individuals in their teens and twenties. While there is no exact profile of cybercriminals due to the variation in offenses noted (see Chapter 1), many offenders appear to be younger individuals (Holt & Bossler, 2014). This may be a positive sign that officers are beginning to recognize the realities of cybercrimes.

In addition, studies have shown officers are unsure who is more often targeted by cybercriminals. For instance, Senjo (2004) found in his sample of Western police officers that only one-third (32 percent) either agreed or strongly agreed that cybercrime occurred more frequently in the corporate world as compared to other places. Only 16 percent of the officers in Holt and Bossler's (2012) study of line officers believed that cybercrime occurred more frequently in corporate settings. In Holt et al.'s (2010) study of FLETC trainees, almost seventy percent (70 percent) believed cybercrime had a greater impact in corporate settings than in home settings. Thus nationwide, officers may perceive that individuals are more likely to be victimized, but the consequences may be greater for corporations.

Perceptions of Cybercrime Uniqueness, Seriousness, and Frequency

Uniqueness

Patrol officers have only recently been surveyed about their perceptions of cybercrime, including its uniqueness, seriousness, and frequency (Holt & Bossler, 2012a; Holt et al., 2010; Senjo, 2004). One of the few studies to our knowledge that examined how the police perceived cybercrime's uniqueness was conducted by Holt and Bossler in 2012. The officers surveyed from this two-city sample were mixed regarding the uniqueness of computer crime. When asked whether they agreed with the following statement, "Computer crime is mostly traditional crime using a computer," 39 percent of the officers agreed. Only one-quarter disagreed, indicating cybercrimes can be distinguished from traditional crime. Interestingly, officers who had received more computer crime training were more likely to view computer crime as similar to traditional crime (Holt & Bossler, 2012a). Thus, officer training appears to be a critical tool to ensure they recognize the similarities between real and virtual crimes and can apply the appropriate investigative skills necessary to each offense type.

Seriousness

Researchers have focused heavily on the perceived severity of cybercrimes among administrators and patrol officers (Bossler & Holt, 2012; Burns et al., 2004; Holt et al., 2010; Holt & Bossler, 2012a). These studies demonstrate that law enforcement does not view cybercrimes in general in the same category of severity as traditional offenses. For instance, Burns et al. (2004) found that 41 percent of law enforcement respondents viewed Internet fraud as a significant societal problem. Bossler and Holt (2012) found that only 28 percent of police officers in their sample disagreed with the statement: "Cybercrime is not taken seriously enough by law enforcement." Half of the officers (49 percent) neither agreed nor disagreed with the statement, suggesting that patrol officers do not think about cybercrime on a daily basis and have few opinions on how to respond to these crimes.

Scholars have also surveyed police officers and representatives about the seriousness of specific cybercrime offenses. One of the first explorations of this topic was Senjo's (2004) study of a sample of Western police officers. When asked to rank the severity of five forms of computer crime, including pedophilia, credit card fraud, electronic theft, copyright infringement, and espionage, officers ranked pedophilia as the most serious form of computer crime, congruent with what previous research on police administrators found (e.g., Stambaugh et al., 2001). Over half (52 percent) of the officers viewed pedophilia as the most serious of the five types provided, followed by credit card fraud, computer espionage, theft of money, and finally copyright infringement.

Although insightful, Senjo (2004) did not provide a definition on what was meant by "serious" to the officers; instead, he had assumed they were thinking about the "threat to life, liberty, and property, and in terms of financial and emotional harm" (p. 62). In addition, his research only compared different forms of computer crime. Since traditional forms of crime were not examined, it did not provide insight on how officers view the seriousness of computer crime in comparison to physical crime.

Expanding on the work of Senjo (2004), Holt and Bossler (2012a) asked police officers to rate on a five-point scale (1 = not serious; 2 = a little serious; 3 = somewhat serious; 4 = serious; 5 = very serious) how serious twelve forms of crime were based on the "financial and emotional harm to victims, and their threat to life, liberty, and personal property" (p. 405). The crimes offered included five traditional offenses (armed robbery, burglary, selling cocaine, shoplifting, and vandalism) and seven computer crimes (copyright infringement such as software and media piracy; credit card fraud; electronic theft of money from accounts; harassment over the Internet; identity theft; pedophilia on the Internet; viruses and malicious software infection). The results in descending order of severity were (means and standard deviations in parentheses): (1) armed robbery (4.83, 0.49); (2) pedophilia on the Internet (4.69; 0.68); (3) burglary (4.56, 0.64); (4) electronic theft of money (4.52, 0.67); (5) identity theft (4.52, 0.65); (6) selling cocaine (4.47, 0.75); (7) credit card fraud (4.42, 0.74); (8) viruses/malicious software (3.93, 0.98); (9) harassment over the Internet (3.58, 1.01); (10) vandalism (3.38, 1.02); (11) copyright infringement (3.37, 1.12); and (12) shoplifting (3.16, 1.04).

These findings demonstrate that real and virtual crimes could be classified into three groups: (1) serious crimes including armed robbery, pedophilia, burglary, electronic theft, identity theft, selling cocaine, and credit card fraud;

(2) moderately serious offenses, including viruses and malicious software infection, and harassment over the Internet; and (3) less serious offenses inclusive of vandalism, copyright infringement, and shoplifting. Holt and Bossler (2012) categorized the offenses into those categories based on medians (not shown) and logical groupings. Armed robbery was ranked as the most severe offense because of its emotional and economic impact on victims, as well as its potential role in homicides. Congruent with previous research based on police administrators and representatives (Hinduja, 2004; Senjo, 2004; Stambaugh et al., 2001), pedophilia was considered the most serious form of cybercrime because it involves the violent and emotional abuse of children (Durkin & Bryant, 1999).

Following child pornography, four serious theft offenses (burglary, identity theft, electronic theft of funds, and credit card fraud) and one serious drug offense (selling cocaine) were grouped together. The categorization suggests patrol officers share the view of many scholars in that some offenses are similar in nature and impact yet occur in different settings (Newman & Clarke, 2003; Wall, 2001). The grouping of serious drugs sales with serious property offenses illustrates that officers perceive the impact of drugs on the individual and the community to be comparable to the financial impact of serious property crimes.

An interesting distinction led malicious software infection to be placed in group two by Holt and Bossler (2012) and not group one. For all group one offenses, 90 percent of the officers saw them as "serious" and half of them viewed them as "very serious." With malicious software infection, however, only one-third (32 percent) of the officers considered malicious software to be very serious, and 72 percent considered it at least serious. Thus, the officers viewed malicious software infection and its consequences as serious, but they did not view it at the same severity level as other serious property offenses. Online harassment was also placed in category two but was not seen as severe as malicious software infection and other crimes. Only one-fifth (19 percent) of the officers considered it as a serious offense, even considering the adverse consequences for youth and adult victims alike (Catalano, 2012; Holt & Bossler, 2009; Reyns et al., 2012).

The final grouping consisted of property offenses in both real (e.g., shoplifting and vandalism) and virtual (e.g., copyright infringement) environments that were considered the least serious by officers. Though these offenses can have significant financial costs, they often affect businesses, public buildings, and large corporations rather than citizens directly. As a result, officers may place less emphasis on offenses that affect large corporations or governments regardless of financial impact (Holt & Bossler, 2012a).

Although these studies illustrate how local patrol officers view cybercrimes, they do not provide insight into the ways specialized cybercrime investigators and digital evidence analysts perceive cybercrime. Holt et al. (2010) surveyed cybercrime investigators and digital evidence handlers who trained with the Federal Law Enforcement Center (FLETC) about offense severity. They asked the officers to rank the severity of sixteen offenses on a scale from least serious (1) to most serious (5). Some of the crimes examined were different from those examined in Holt and Bossler's previously discussed study (2012), preventing a complete comparison. The sixteen offenses in order from most serious to least serious in the eyes of FLETC trainees were (means reported in parentheses): (1) child pornography (4.86); (2) physical terrorist attacks (4.84); (3) cyberterrorism (4.59); (4) selling hard drugs (4.49); (5) electronic theft of money (4.46); (6) viruses/malicious software (4.20); (7) hitting someone without a reason (3.88); (8) viewing electronic data (3.85); (9) breaking in a vehicle or building (3.82); (10) harassment over the Internet (3.68); (11) vandalism (3.34); (12) software piracy (3.26); (13) stealing more than $50 (3.19); (14) media piracy (2.97); (15) unauthorized wireless use (2.29); and (16) stealing less than $5 (2.09).

The FLETC trainees believed that child pornography and sexual solicitation of minors were the most serious forms of crime, congruent with previous research (Holt & Bossler, 2012a; Stambaugh et al., 2010). The inclusion of items on terrorist attacks against both physical and electronic targets (i.e., cyberterror) illustrated that these officers and agents attending FLETC training considered terrorist attacks against physical targets to be the second most serious offense, second only to child pornography. In addition, both forms of terrorist attacks received relatively similar scores. The trainees viewed selling hard drugs as more serious than did the patrol officers (Holt & Bossler, 2012a). The high scores for drug offenses support the notion officers still view these offenses as highly damaging to communities. They also see the links to serious forms of disorder and violence (Harocopos & Hough, 2005). These trainees also appreciated the seriousness of electronic theft and malicious software infection. In comparing these findings from Holt et al. (2010) and Holt and Bossler (2012), it is in the middle categories in which the most variation can be found. These scores also indicate that the officers still viewed violence, even if it was virtual such as online harassment, to be more serious than physical forms of property crimes. Similar to previous studies, lesser forms of property crime, whether physical or virtual in nature, were seen as equal and the least serious.

Frequency

Previous studies have also examined officer perceptions about the frequency of cybercrimes. Surveying officers about their perceptions of the frequency of offenses is not intended as a measure of how often they actually occur, but rather as an assessment of their views on these problems. Since official statistics and calls for service on cybercrimes are scant at this time, these measures provide a point of comparison between their perceptions of the frequency of traditional and computer crimes.

Holt and Bossler (2012) asked the Savannah and Charlotte officers to rate how frequent (1 = rare, 2 = somewhat rare, 3 = somewhat frequent, 4 = frequent, 5 = very frequent) the same twelve offenses occurred that were scored on severity. The offenses in order of perceived frequency from most to least frequent were (means in parentheses): (1) burglary (4.55); (2) selling cocaine (4.51); (3) shoplifting (4.51); (4) armed robbery (4.30); (5) vandalism (4.17); (6) credit card fraud (4.16); (7) identity theft (3.91); (8) electronic theft of money (3.83); (9) pedophilia on the Internet (3.82); (10) viruses (3.78); (11) copyright infringement (3.69); and (12) harassment over the Internet (3.59). These findings indicated that the top five most frequently perceived offenses were all traditional offenses rather than cybercrimes. Offenses such as malicious software infections, online harassment, and copyright infringement, however, all occur more frequently than traditional offenses (e.g., Business Software Alliance, 2012; Symantec, 2013). This would mean that officers' perceptions are not congruent with reality and may influence their desire to appropriately respond to these frequent and serious crimes. These views may stem from the underreporting of cybercrime, and a lack of personal experience with cybercrime calls for service (Bossler & Holt, 2012; Wall, 2001).

In Holt et al.'s (2010) study of attendees at FLETC training in the late 2000s, the respondents rated eight cybercrime offenses on how frequent they perceived those offenses occurring on a scale of 1 (never) to 6 (very frequently). The least perceived frequent cybercrime that occurred was any form of terrorist attack against electronic targets (cyberterror). The attendees still saw this offense occurring frequently, however, as the mean score for this offense was 4.58. The specific scores were (means in parentheses): (1) terrorist attacks against electronic targets (cyberterror) (4.58); (2) viewing someone else's electronic data without permission (4.83); (3) electronic theft of money from accounts (4.96); (4) harassment over the Internet (5.10); (5) viruses and malicious software infection (5.11); (6) child pornography and sexual solicitation (5.35); (7) unauthorized copying of software (5.38); and (8) unauthorized copying of media (5.54). In a way, the scores only differentiate whether they perceive the offenses as occurring frequently or very frequently. These scores, however, also reflect that officers perceive media and software piracy to be occurring the most frequently, although they believe that they are the least serious cybercrime offenses. Child pornography, the cybercrime viewed as the most serious, is perceived as occurring very frequently and only occurring less often than different types of piracy. This finding is in contrast to cyber-attacks which they consider to be very serious but occurring the least often.

Assessing Specialized Officers' Perceptions of Cybercrime

To examine how computer crime trainees perceive cybercrime, we administered a survey to a population of 1,701 law enforcement officers who completed a computer training program through the National White Collar Crime Center (NW3C). This training was provided to anyone whose agency had some interest or mission related to cybercrime that required additional training. The NW3C sent an e-mail invitation with a link to an online survey in March 2009, identifying the research team and the NW3C staff assisting the project. A total of 292 individuals responded to the survey, which is a low response rate (about 17 percent) but consistent with the overall trend of declining survey response rates (Bickart & Schmittlein, 1999; Dey, 1997; Sheehan, 2001).

Seriousness

Respondents rated the seriousness of 15 items on a five-point scale from one (least serious) to five (most serious), including six traditional offenses and nine cybercrime-related offenses. As Table 2.1 indicates, officers attending computer crime training programs considered child pornography and cyberterrorism to be the most serious offenses. Ninety percent of the officers considered child pornography to be most serious while 65 percent felt cyberterrorism to be the most serious. These trainees also rated hard drugs as the third most serious offense, above serious property crimes. Table 2.1 also illustrates the officers felt two serious forms of cybercrime—electronic theft of money and malicious software infection—to be more serious than hitting someone without a reason. Thus, these officers clearly see not only the financial, but also an emotional, impact that these cybercrimes have on individuals, families, and businesses.

Respondents viewed breaking into a home or vehicle and viewing electronic data to be relatively similar in terms of severity. Similar to previous research (Holt & Bossler, 2012a), these analyses indicate that officers view electronic harassment to be more serious than many forms of more minor property crimes, including vandalism and piracy. The least serious offenses were all property-related. Software piracy, media piracy, and unauthorized access of a wireless account were viewed as similar to stealing more than $50 while stealing less than $5 was identified as the least serious offense by respondents (see also Holt & Bossler, 2012a; Holt et al., 2010).

To test whether these findings were robust, we examined how they varied by age, sex, race, the total number of officers within the agency, years in law enforcement, experience with digital evidence or investigating computer crimes, and training. Older trainees were more likely to believe that all crimes in general were more serious than younger officers. In particular, older officers felt five real world crimes were more serious than their younger counterparts: selling hard drugs ($r = 0.120$), stealing less than $5 ($r = 0.127$), burglary ($r = 0.142$), stealing more than $50 ($r = 0.169$), and hitting someone without a reason ($r = 0.183$). Older officer viewed five cybercrimes as more serious, including using someone else's wireless connection without authorization ($r = 0.127$), harassment over the Internet ($r = 0.141$), media piracy ($r = 0.160$), viruses and malicious software infection ($r = 0.165$), and software piracy ($r = 0.199$).

Female respondents felt three cybercrimes—electronic theft, viruses and malicious software infection, and wireless connection theft—were more serious than their male counterparts. Non-White trainees provided significantly higher seriousness scores for all but three offenses: child pornography, software piracy, and electronic theft of money from accounts. Officers who were in agencies with more officers found eight of the offenses to be more serious than officers coming from smaller agencies—viewing someone else's electronic data ($r = 0.123$), using someone else's wireless connection without authorization ($r = 0.124$), viruses/malicious software infection ($r = 0.143$), harassment over the Internet ($r = 0.157$), hitting someone without reason ($r = 0.163$), burglary ($r = 0.164$), stealing something worth more than $50 ($r = 0.172$), and vandalism ($r = 0.189$).

Officers with more years of law enforcement experienced reported hitting someone without a reason ($r = 0.131$) and software piracy ($r = 0.139$) were more serious than officers with fewer years on the job. Trainees who were sworn officers thought that child pornography and cyberterrorism were more serious than non-sworn officers. Officers with more years of digital experience handling and/or computer crime investigating, however, found all of the offenses to be less serious except for child pornography and cyberterrorism. Finally, officers who receive more annual training believed that 12 of the offenses were less serious than officers who received less training, with the exception of viewing someone else's electronic data, child pornography, and cyberterrorism.

The officers' perceptions of the severity of cybercrime demonstrate that they placed little emphasis on minor forms of theft, whether on or off-line (Holt & Bossler, 2012a; Holt et al., 2010; Senjo, 2004). Electronic theft, however, was viewed as a much more serious form of cybercrime than any type of digital piracy. In addition, officers understood that malicious software infection was a serious issue in that it can lead to other major forms of victimization, such as theft, computer intrusions, or cyber-attacks (Bossler & Holt, 2009; Brenner, 2008; Taylor et al., 2010). In addition, the emphasis placed on both physical and cyberterror attacks suggests that there is a need to improve response capabilities for local first responders in the event of an incident (Holt et al., 2010). Finally, the seriousness of child pornography in the eyes of law enforcement is consistent with previous research regardless of the city or year in which the study was conducted (Holt et al., 2010; Holt & Bossler, 2012a; Senjo, 2004; Stambaugh et al., 2001).

Table 2.1: NW3C Trainees Views on Seriousness of Crime

Crime	Mean	SD	Least 1	2	3	4	Most 5
(1) Child pornography	4.86	0.48	0.4	0.4	2.2	6.9	90.2
(2) Cyberterrorism	4.53	0.73	0.0	1.4	9.4	24.3	64.9
(3) Selling hard drugs	4.36	0.78	0.4	1.4	12.3	33.6	52.3
(4) Electronic theft of money	4.30	0.75	0.0	1.4	13.4	39.1	46.0
(5) Viruses/malicious software infection	3.90	0.99	1.1	7.6	25.5	32.4	33.5
(6) Hitting someone w/o reason	3.87	0.95	1.4	5.8	26.7	36.8	29.2
(7) Viewing electronic data	3.82	0.94	0.7	7.9	27.0	37.8	26.6
(8) Breaking in vehicle/building to steal	3.65	0.96	1.8	8.4	33.1	36.4	20.4
(9) Harassment over Internet	3.60	0.98	0.7	12.6	33.6	32.1	20.9
(10) Vandalism	3.34	1.02	3.6	16.5	36.0	30.2	13.7
(11) Software piracy	2.95	1.19	12.3	23.6	34.4	16.7	13.0
(12) Stealing more than $50	2.86	1.09	7.6	34.4	31.9	16.3	9.8
(13) Unauthorized Wireless Use	2.85	1.26	18.7	19.1	33.5	16.2	12.6
(14) Media piracy	2.82	1.27	17.0	25.6	29.2	14.4	13.7
(15) Stealing less than $5	1.92	1.23	54.2	18.5	14.9	5.8	6.5

Frequency

Respondents were then asked to assess their perceptions of the frequency with which cybercrimes occurred. The findings displayed in Table 2.2 support the findings of Holt et al.'s (2010) work a few years earlier. Officers perceived that various forms of piracy occurred the most frequently, followed by what they considered the most serious form of cybercrime—child pornography. The trainees saw the following offenses occurring from most to least frequent: malicious software infection, online harassment, electronic theft of money from accounts, viewing electronic data, and cyberterrorism. Though there is not sufficient statistical evidence from law enforcement sources, general research suggests that respondent perceptions correspond to the tremendously high rate of piracy worldwide (Business Software Alliance, 2012) and the substantial number of arrests for child exploitation crimes by local and federal law enforcement in the U.S. (Jones et al., 2013). Thus, the respondents' perceptions may be relatively accurate compared to existing evidence of cybercrime trends.

Table 2.2: NW3C Trainees Perceptions on the Frequency of Cybercrime

Crime	Mean	SD	Never (0)	Rarely (1)	Occasionally (2)	Frequently (3)	Very Frequently (4)
Media piracy	3.61	0.73	0.7	2.2	3.6	21.8	71.6
Software piracy	3.54	0.77	0.7	2.5	5.1	25.0	66.7
Child pornography and sexual solicitation	3.46	0.69	0.4	0.7	6.9	36.7	55.3
Viruses/malicious software	3.24	0.89	1.1	3.6	13.1	34.2	48.0
Harassment over the Internet	3.20	0.89	0.4	4.4	16.1	33.2	46.0
Electronic theft of money from accounts	3.08	0.89	0.4	4.0	21.8	34.9	38.9
Viewing electronic data	2.93	0.87	0.7	5.1	21.7	45.7	26.8
Cyberterrorism	2.69	1.04	1.1	13.8	26.4	32.6	26.1

We conducted analyses to identify significant differences among the officers based on sex, race, and the amount of annual training. Female trainees viewed child pornography and cyberterrorism as more frequent offenses than their male counterparts. Non-White respondents also perceived child pornography, electronic theft of money from accounts, viruses and malicious software infection, and cyberterrorism as more frequent. Respondents coming from larger agencies perceived crime in general as occurring more frequently than trainees from smaller agencies. Finally, officers who received more annual training perceived cyberterrorism as occurring less frequently than officers with less training.

Summary and Conclusions

This chapter demonstrates that there is a substantial dark figure of cybercrime that currently exists. There are few available official data sources that can be used to assess the scope of cybercrimes, such as NIBRS, though this data is limited because of the ways that agencies can report offenses. Self-report data from the Internet Crime Complaint Center provides an alternative assessment, but is oriented toward financial rather than person-based cybercrimes. As a consequence, there is a need for dramatic improvements in the documentation of cybercrime calls for service and victimization data.

Despite these limitations, the population of NW3C trainees sampled appeared to recognize there are distinct differences in the severity of cybercrimes based on their harm to individuals or property. Their perceptions on the severity of cyberterrorism and child pornography relative to offenses such as piracy are sensible given the clear differences in the scope of injury that may result from these offenses relative to the limited economic harm caused by pirated music or movie consumption. At the same time, their responses suggested that they are aware of the massive rate of piracy relative to uncommon incidents like cyberterrorism. The responses also demonstrated that law enforcement appears to better understand the scope of cybercrime compared to survey-based studies from the early 2000s (e.g., Hinduja, 2003; Senjo, 2004). Given the trainees' perceptions of cybercrime, there is a need to understand how officers view the value of cybercrime training and their roles in dealing with these cases. These issues will be explored in Chapter 3 to improve our understanding of the response to cybercrime.

Chapter 3

Examining the Attitudes of Local Law Enforcement toward Cybercrime Training

As noted in Chapter 2, there is a definitive dark figure of cybercrime that plagues our understanding of these offenses. If citizens do not report cybercrimes to the police with considerable frequency, it is plausible that officers may interpret this as evidence that cybercrimes are not a problem in their area. Furthermore, officer perceptions about how cybercrimes operate may lead them to feel this is a crime best suited for federal investigation (e.g., Senjo, 2004). If law enforcement management does not discuss cybercrime reporting issues or threats, then this may exacerbate the perception of cybercrime as a non-existent problem at the local level (e.g., Holt & Bossler, 2012a).

Since officer attitudes toward cybercrime may be affected by various internal and external factors to their department, it is important to consider how they view the value of cybercrime training. Cases involving computer hacking, harassment, or child exploitation involve unique pieces of evidence and information that may not be gathered in the same fashion as a crime in the physical world. As a result, officers must have some understanding of these cases to effectively respond to calls for service. If they see no value in cybercrime investigation or have preconceived notions about the challenges or difficulties inherent to these crimes, then they may be less interested in investigating cybercrimes from the outset (e.g., Goodman, 1997; Holt & Bossler, 2012a).

Few researchers, however, have considered either the issue of officer interest in cybercrime training or the distribution of resources designed to address the problem of cybercrime at the local level. This chapter will address both of these issues using empirical research. First, we consider the distribution of specialized cybercrime task forces and special units across the U.S. Second, we examine officer interest in receiving additional cybercrime investigative training and participating in future cybercrime investigations as well as the factors that may drive their reported interest in general computer training.

Investigative Resources for Cybercrime Cases

Given that the commission of cybercrime can be sophisticated and require evidence collection and analysis techniques beyond what may immediately be available for traditional offenses, it is not surprising many police departments feel such cases are better suited to specialized units or taskforces. These terms refer to distinct organizational forms, though they may have a common focus on a given form of crime. A special unit may serve a specific role in dealing with either single forms of crime or unique populations (e.g., juveniles). A task force, however, can incorporate officers from various agencies at the local, state, and/or federal level to investigate crimes that cut across jurisdictional boundaries.

Cybercrimes are a key example of such an offense, as an offender may easily reside in a county or state far from their victim. In particular, there has been an increasing amount of local police department resources devoted to cybercrime investigation, especially those involving the exploitation of children (e.g., Marcum et al., 2010; Wolak, Finkelhor, & Mitchell, 2012). Substantial resources have been invested in a unique task force strategy operating primarily at the local level. The creation of Internet Crimes Against Children (ICAC) task forces provide a mechanism for coordination of resources among local law enforcement, prosecutors, and federal agencies (ICAC, 2014).

The program began in 1998 under mandate from the Office of Juvenile Justice and Delinquency Prevention (OJJDP) to improve the resources available to combat youth victimization at all levels of law enforcement, including investigative resources, forensic and technological assistance, and prosecutorial guidance. In fact, there is now a regular schedule of digital forensic and investigative training for ICAC investigators offered across the country, which are supported by various federal agencies (ICAC, 2014). The ICAC program is currently comprised of 61 task forces, operating in every state in the nation. Some states with larger populations and geography have multiple ICACs, such as Florida, California, and Texas (ICAC, 2014).

The spread and presence of ICACs have increased the number of arrests for child exploitation crimes across the country (Marcum & Higgins, 2011; Wolak et al., 2012). For instance, a survey using a nationally representative sample of over 2,500 local and federal law enforcement agencies suggests arrests for technology-facilitated child exploitation crimes has increased substantially since 2000. The number of arrests for child-related crimes increased threefold since 2000, when there were 2,577 arrests for child sexual exploitation crimes in 2000 to 8,144 in 2009 (Wolak et al., 2012). Similar evidence has been found within surveys of local law enforcement agencies, regardless of their relationship to an ICAC, indicating most cybercrime investigations at the local level focus on sexual offenses rather than financial or property-related crimes (Burns et al., 2004; Hinduja, 2004; Holt et al., 2010; Senjo, 2004).

Though ICACs appear to expand enforcement of child exploitation crimes, few studies consider how local and state agencies respond to cybercrimes. Task forces are a logical solution as they promote resource sharing and improve jurisdictional coordination for investigation. In fact, the National Institute of Justice identified the formation of task forces as a critical priority to improve the capability of state and local cybercrime investigators in 2001 (Stambaugh et al., 2001). Currently, it is unclear whether most local law enforcement agencies use these structures or simply designate officers to investigate these crimes.

These questions can be addressed through an examination of survey data conducted by the Law Enforcement Management and Administrative Statistics (LEMAS). The LEMAS survey covers a nationally representative sample of approximately 3,000 agencies and boasts a 90 percent response rate. Agencies include municipal and county police, sheriffs, primary state agencies, and tribal and regional police. The LEMAS survey collects organizational and administrative data on state and local law enforcement agencies across the United States every three to four years (BJS, 2012). The survey asks about various aspects of the department, such as number of employees (sworn and civilian), salaries, budgets, training, employment requirements, special units, and policies.

Germaine to the question of cybercrime resources, the LEMAS survey in 2003 asked two specific questions: (1) " ... Did your agency have PRIMARY responsibility for or perform on a regular basis during the 12-month period ending June 30, 2003 ... criminal investigation for cybercrime?"; and (2) "How does your agency address the following problems/tasks—cybercrime?" The response option for the first question was a checkbox for "yes." The response options for the second question were: (1) agency has specialized unit with full-time personnel to address problem, (2) agency has dedicated personnel to address this problem, (3) agency addresses this problem, but doesn't have dedicated personnel, and (4) agency does not address this problem. The survey asked about the second question on cybercrime only in the 2007 survey to large agencies with 100 or more officers. While these survey items provide little detail about the resources dedicated to the problem of cybercrime, they do allow us to understand how departments were at least addressing the problem.

In 2003, 62 percent of municipal and county police departments indicated they had primary responsibility for cybercrime (n = 1,926). For primary state agencies (typically the state police), 53 percent of those agencies indicated they

Table 3.1: The Number of Agencies Reporting Cybercrime Investigation as a Primary Responsibility by Agency Type and Number of Sworn Officers in 2003

Size of Agency by Sworn Officers

Agency Type	1–9	10–49	50–99	100 or more	Total (n)
Municipal/County Police	11.1%	34.0%	19.0%	35.8%	100% (1,918)
Sheriff's Departments	10.8%	33.8%	12.9%	42.5%	100% (863)
Primary State Agency	N/A	N/A	N/A	100.0%	100% (49)
Totals	10.9%	33.4%	17.0%	38.7%	100% (2,830)

had primary responsibility in this area. Further, among the 863 sheriff's departments, 56 percent indicated they had primary responsibility. Overall, there was little difference in the percent of municipal/county police, sheriffs, or primary state agencies that had primary responsibility for cybercrime investigations.

When cybercrime as a primary investigation responsibility in 2003 is broken down by agency size, differences exist. Table 3.1 shows the percent differences in the number of agencies reporting cybercrime as a primary investigative function across the types of agencies by the number of paid, sworn officers. Not surprising, larger departments report a higher percentage of responding agencies with cybercrime investigation responsibility as a primary function. This same pattern of rising percentages of agencies was also true as the population of the jurisdiction increased, given that department size and size of a jurisdiction are highly correlated (Hickman & Reaves, 2006). Note, however, that the category of agencies with 10 to 49 sworn officers is more similar to the 100 or more sworn officer category than smaller agencies (except for state agencies, which only have such responsibilities reported in the largest size category). This is true when the distribution is broken down across agency types (the last row in Table 3.1).

Turning to the second question regarding how the agency addressed the problem of cybercrime, about 11 percent of responders in 2003 did not formally address the problem (n = 101), similar to the percentage of agencies in 2007 (9 percent) reporting that they did not formally address the problem (n = 81). About 26 percent (n = 237) of respondents had specialized units and 29 percent had dedicated personnel but no special unit. About a third of responders (34 percent or 307 agencies) addressed the problem, but had no unit or personnel. In 2007, of those agencies that did address the problem, 37 percent had a specialized unit will full-time personnel (n = 329), a substantial increase from 2003. Thirty-one percent had no unit, but did designate personnel to the problem (n = 271). Further, 23 percent addressed the problem but did not designate personnel (n = 203), a significant decrease from 34 percent of agencies in 2003.

Based on the LEMAS survey, many agencies devote resources to investigating cybercrime, especially in larger organizations. These statistics do not inform us, however, of how departments and officers perceive the seriousness of cybercrime (see Chapter 2 for discussion of officer perceptions of cybercrime), nor do they explain perceptions on the necessity to devote resources to the problem (see Chapter 4 for officer perceptions on strategy). The LEMAS data also do not tell us the future outlook: do department leaders believe more resources should be devoted to cybercrime?

A study by the Police Executive Research Forum (PERF), who also sponsors the LEMAS survey along with the Bureau of Justice Statistics, reported on technological needs of law enforcement agencies regarding the investigation of cybercrime (Koper et al., 2009). According to the 2009 PERF study, about 90 percent of the approximately 300 PERF-affiliated agencies agreed that the 'prevention and investigation of electronic/cybercrime' was an operational area that will have high priority in the next three to five years. Compare that with about 62 percent that agreed organized crime was a future priority or the 64 percent that agreed that homeland security threats and terrorism were a future priority. In fact, electronic/cybercrime investigation was ranked sixth among 20 items based on the percent that agreed. In addition, the PERF study authors did a literature review and found that the detection, prevention, and investigation of cyber-attacks were a consistent concern among respondents in other studies of technology and policing. Another finding from the PERF study was that 53 percent of responding agencies indicated they had cyber forensic equipment and 10 percent indicated they were likely to acquire it (2009, p. 43).

Officer Interest in Cybercrime Training

Because police departments devote some resources to cybercrime investigation, it begs the question how well officers train to respond to these cases. Many researchers and scholars have indicated patrol officers must respond to cybercrime calls in the same way they would a traditional crime, including securing evidence, speaking with witnesses, and developing information (Bossler & Holt, 2012; Hinduja, 2007; NIJ, 2008; Stambaugh et al., 2001). The quality of a first responder's scene management has a dramatic impact on the likelihood a real world crime is solved (Hinduja, 2007). It is likely that the same conditions apply to cybercrime cases though few have assessed the knowledge base of line officers and the quality of their training to properly handle cybercrime calls (Hinduja, 2007; Holt et al., 2010).

Though NIJ (2008) and other agencies (US Secret Service, 2013) have developed digital-evidence training manuals and pocket guides, access to these materials does not ensure success in the field. The range of crime types and evidence that may be present requires some insights by responding officers to recognize, seize, document, handle, package, and transport evidence. As a result, additional training ensures first responders can appropriately handle any cybercrime scene. In their national assessment, Stambaugh and associates (2001), for example, found 37 percent of local agencies provided basic computer crime awareness and evidence collection training for their front-line personnel. Similarly, Hinduja (2004) found 75 percent of Michigan law enforcement agencies viewed additional training for front-line officers as the primary solution to handle effectively cybercrime cases.

A range of factors limits training availability, such as operating budgets and the total available agency manpower (Hinduja, 2007; Holt et al., 2010). Smaller agencies may not have a single officer dedicated to cybercrime investigation. Agency administrators may view funding cybercrime training as a low priority relative to other offenses. To that end, Holt and associates (2010) found the majority of agencies in a national sample of local law enforcement had fewer than 20 percent of their officers trained in digital evidence handling (79.3 percent of the sample) or online crime investigation (88.1 percent of the sample). However, the number of trained personnel may improve the success of any investigation. Research by Marcum and Higgins (2011) found that a larger number of trained personnel on ICAC task forces correlated with an increase in the number of investigations involving computer forensics.

To that end, cybercrime training varies in the kinds of crimes covered in the coursework. While police academies might provide some basic cybercrime information, the federal government provides training in cybercrime through a variety of sources. One of the most prominent groups engaged in cybercrime investigation training is the National White Collar Crime Center (NW3C). The NW3C courses provide training in two areas: cyber investigation and cyber forensics. The courses cover topics on identifying and seizing electronic evidence, cell phone investigation, data recovery, network investigations, and forensic analysis. The courses offer basic, intermediate, and advanced instruction and are free for state, local, or tribal agencies. Many courses have restrictions, such as requiring a basic course first or only offering to officers affiliated with a particular task force (e.g., the Internet Crimes Against Children Task Force).

Given the dearth of information on the availability and use of training services, we worked with the NW3C to administer a survey to a sample of 1,701 law enforcement officers who completed their computer-training program. This training was provided to anyone whose agency had some interest or mission related to cybercrime that required additional training. The NW3C sent an e-mail invitation with a link to an online survey in March 2009, identifying the research team and the NW3C staff assisting the project. A total of 292 individuals responded to the survey, which is a low response rate (about 17 percent) but consistent with the overall trend of declining survey response rates (Bickart & Schmittlein, 1999; Dey, 1997; Sheehan, 2001). Due to missing data, 285 completed surveys were used, including respondents who were police officers, detectives, supervisors, crime technicians, or had other roles in law enforcement agencies.

One of the questions asked of the trainees was, "About how many weeks do you attend job training per year?" The response options were: (1) less than one week; (2) one week; (3) two weeks; (4) three weeks; and (5) four or more weeks. Of the 283 who responded, the modal category was two weeks with a little more than a quarter of the respondents (28 percent), followed by 23 percent of the respondents who reported one week. Twenty-two percent received four or more weeks, about 18 percent received three weeks, and 10 percent received less than one week of training per year.

To better understand the variation in cybercrime training throughout the year, we conducted both univariate and multivariate analyses. The predictors used to examine training were: age (measured continuously); sex (female = 1); race (non-White = 1); and education (measured ordinally (1) high school/GED; (2) some college; (3) two-year degree; (4) four-year degree; (5) graduate degree). We also included the number of officers in the agency, measured ordinally: (0) 50 or fewer; (1) 51 to 250; (2) 251 to 1,000; (3) 1,001 to 3,500; (4) more than 3,500; whether the officer was sworn (unsworn = 1); and years of digital evidence handling or cybercrime investigation experience, measured ordinally (0) 0; (1) 1–2 years; (2) 3–4 years; (3) 5 or more years. See Table 3.2 for descriptives.

Bivariate analyses indicated a few measures were correlated to the dependent measure (full results not shown). In the following results, we only report

Table 3.2: Descriptive Statistics for NW3C Predictors of Weeks of Job Training

	Mean	Std. Dev.	Min.	Max.	N
Dependent Variable:					
1) Weeks of job training	3.19	1.28	1	5	283
Block 1: Demographics:					
1) Age	42.23	8.75	24	65	283
2) Female	0.13	0.34	0	1	285
3) Non-White	0.18	0.39	0	1	282
4) Education	3.51	1.16	1	5	284
5) No. Officers in agency	1.70	1.49	0	4	285
6) Unsworn	0.09	0.28	0	1	283
7) Digital experience	1.24	1.21	0	3	284

significant results unless otherwise noted.[1] Older officers (r = -0.153) received less training. Having more experience with handling digital evidence was significantly correlated with receiving more training (r = 0.187). Although females did not report receiving less training than males, non-White (mean = 2.73) respondents reported receiving less training than Whites (mean = 3.29).

The univariate analyses suggested further multivariate examination might provide further insight. Due to the ordinal nature of the dependent variable, we ran ordered logistic regression (see Table 3.3 for detail). A regression is an analytic technique that predicts the effect of one variable upon another, hold-

---

1. A correlation is a measure of association between two variables, evaluated on a scale of 0.00, or no association, to 1.00 a perfect association. A correlation can be either positive (as case values increase for one variable, they increase on the other variable) or negative (the case values change inversely). If two variables have a perfect association, then you would be able to predict the value of one variable knowing the other; for a zero association (or r = 0.000), you could not predict the value of one variable knowing the value of another variable. Thus, the larger the r value, the stronger the association and the better the predicted relationship. Another statistical factor to consider is significance. If the relationship between two variables is statistically significant, then we can be reasonably sure that the results we observe in the sample would reoccur if we conducted the same study with a different sample. When results are not statistically significant, researchers assume random errors in the data cause the observed results. In the following results, we only report significant results unless otherwise noted.

Table 3.3: Ordered Logistic Regression Model Predicting Annual Training

Variables	Estimate	SE
Age	-0.039*	0.013
Female	0.058	0.330
Non-White	-0.978*	0.310
Education	0.057	0.095
# of officers	0.185*	0.081
Unsworn	-0.352	0.381
Digital experience	0.333*	0.094
-2LL		810.642
χ^2 (7)		31.602
Nagelkerke R^2		0.114
N		275

Notes: * $p \leq 0.05$; ** $p \leq 0.01$
SE is standard error for the regression coefficients

ing all other predictors at a constant level. Thus, we were able to isolate the impact of one particular predictor upon the outcome variable.[2]

After holding experience with digital evidence and the size of the department constant, older officers and non-White officers received significantly less annual training than their younger and White colleagues. In addition, respondents who were employed by larger agencies received more annual training than officers in smaller agencies. This is sensible given that larger agencies typically have greater financial resources to provide specialized training and staff task forces (e.g., Wall, 2007). Finally, officers who had more years experience of handling digital evidence or working on cybercrime cases received more weeks of training throughout the year. Those officers who have basic skills for analysis and experience in the field may be better suited to receive specialized training that would otherwise be beyond the comprehension of new staff (see Ferraro & Casey, 2005), which may account for this relationship.

---

2. The proportional odds assumption held for the model (χ^2 31.138 (21), p = .071). Multicollinearity was not a problem as no VIF exceeded 10 and tolerance levels were above 0.2.

The previous analysis suggests unique demographic and agency factors affect which individuals receive more cybercrime investigation training than others. Larger agencies and those with young officers may have greater economic resources to provide more training. These conditions are not, however, present across the majority of local law enforcement agencies in the U.S. Consequently, we need to understand how line officers perceive the value of cybercrime training and gauge any desire to receive these resources.

Officer Attitudes toward Training

Limited research has examined whether line officers desire cybercrime training or want to participate in these investigations (Holt & Bossler, 2012b). The lack of empirical investigation on this issue is not surprising given the generally small body of research focusing on policing cybercrime generally. To date one of the only studies to address this issue was conducted by Holt and Bossler (2012b) using a population of respondents from two southeastern U.S. cities. They found that 40 percent of their sample was interested in conducting cybercrime investigations, and 57.7 percent expressed interest in cybercrime investigation training.

The authors examined the factors associated with officer interest in training and investigation and found several consistent demographic and attitudinal predictors. Specifically, older officers who had greater computer proficiency and no prior computer training were more likely to be interested in training (Holt & Bossler, 2012b). In addition, officers who saw value in cybercrime investigation and felt that these offenses would change the nature of policing were more likely to desire training and investigative roles. An officer's exposure to cybercrime-related calls for service was not, however, associated with any interest in training or investigation. Thus, it is plausible that the attitudes and ability of an officer are more valuable in determining who is an appropriate candidate for cybercrime training than basing choices on rank or perceived experience in the field (Holt & Bossler, 2012b).

Because there has been such limited research on the issue of training among local law enforcement officers, there is a need to examine what factors may directly influence officer willingness to receive various forms of computer and cybercrime training. To that end, we collected survey data from patrol officers in two southeastern cities in the U.S.: the Charlotte-Mecklenburg police department (CMPD) in Charlotte, North Carolina and the Savannah-Chatham Metropolitan police department (SCMPD) in Savannah, Georgia. Though these cities share regional commonalities, they differ on several key characteristics. Charlotte is a large city with approximately 687,456 residents in the city limits and over two million in the combined statistical area, compared with Savannah's smaller population of 134,669 residents (U.S. Census Bureau, 2009). Charlotte is also a key banking and financial hub, while Savannah's economy is driven by tourism, shipping, and the military. The population of Savannah is also largely African-American (57 percent) while Charlotte's largest racial group is White (55 percent).

These two cities' police departments varied in both size and officer demographics. The CMPD had over 1,400 patrol officers while the SCMPD had just fewer than 400 patrol officers during the study period of Spring 2008. Though 85 percent of the officers in both departments were male, 78 percent of Charlotte's department was White, compared to Savannah's department, which was 59 percent White. Charlotte also has a specialized computer crime task force, which did not exist in the Savannah department.

The survey instrument used for this study was created using questions adapted from studies focusing on computer crime awareness among the general public (Furnell, 2002) and law enforcement (Hinduja, 2004; Senjo, 2004; Stambaugh et al., 2001). This survey was distributed to all patrol officers at the rank of Sergeant and below in order to capture the attitudes of patrol officers rather than management. In the SCMPD, paper copies of the survey instrument were given to command staff at the weekly departmental meeting in spring 2008 and then distributed to patrol officers. The command staff returned 144 completed surveys (36 percent response rate) back to the research team. In Charlotte, 124 officers completed the survey, giving an overall response rate of 9 percent. The majority were male (87 percent) and White (84 percent), which resembles the demographic characteristics of police officers in U.S. police departments (LEMAS, 2010). In keeping with the demographics of the two departments, the percentages of male officers in the two samples were equivalent but Charlotte had more White officers than did Savannah.

The officers in both samples were asked how they much agreed (1 = strongly disagree, 2 = disagree, 3 = neither agree nor disagree, 4 = agree, 5 = strongly agree) with the following statement, "I am interested in receiving general computer training (e.g., Word, programming, Internet)" (see Table 3.4 for descriptives; Holt & Bossler, 2012b). The mean response for this statement was somewhat neutral at 3.60. Surprisingly, this response was comparable to that of officer interest in cybercrime investigation training. The difference between the two items is that a larger percentage of the officers (28 percent) were not sure whether they were interested in cybercrime investigation training. Considering that only 40 percent of the officers were interested in participating in

Table 3.4: Interest in Cybercrime Training Among Patrol Officers in Two Southeastern Cities

	Mean	Std. dev.	Min.	Max.	SD	D	Neither	A	SA
Computer training	3.60	1.15	1	5	5.2%	15.5%	17.1%	39.3%	23.0%
Cybercrime investigation training	3.58	1.01	1	5	3.2%	11.5%	27.75%	39.5%	18.2%
Future cybercrime investigations	3.17	1.11	1	5	7.6%	19.5%	33.55%	27.1%	12.4%

future cybercrime investigations, it would appear that line officers are more interested in training rather than the actual investigations of cybercrimes.

Officer desire for basic computer training was significantly correlated with cybercrime investigation training (r = 0.525) and participating in future cybercrime investigations (r = 0.396). These interests were not as strongly related as the correlation between interest in cybercrime-investigation training and conducting cybercrime investigations (r = 0.722). Thus, these items measure three separate interests in technology training and cannot be arbitrarily used on their own as indicators of interest in cybercrime investigation (see also Holt & Bossler, 2012b).

The survey included two other items to assess officer interest in basic computer training (see Table 3.5 for descriptives). These other two items were: (1) "Although learning new computer skills might be helpful, I would rather receive additional training in something else" (Reverse coded, 1 = strongly agree to 5 = strongly disagree); and (2) "Additional computer training should be a top priority for our department" (1 = strongly disagree to 5 = strongly agree). These two items along with the variable for interest in computer training were used to create a scale for general interest in cybercrime investigation (α = 0.693).[3]

In order to identify which officers were more interested in general computer training, we used the scaled item described above as the dependent variable and created six blocks of independent variables. These variables include: (1) demographics; (2) cybercrime exposure; (3) computer training; (4) computer proficiency; (5) perceptions of the Internet and cybercrime; and (6) views on policing cybercrime. All descriptive statistics are presented in Table 3.5.

---

3. Researchers use a scale to combine several measures into one, assuming the separate measures are all highly correlated. Researchers assess this assumption through a statistic called coefficient alpha, which should be about 0.700 or greater on a scale of 0.000 to 1.000.

Block 1: Demographics. Demographic measures examined were: *sex* (1 = Female); *black* (1 = Black); *other race* (1 = Race other than Black or White); *age* (measured continuously); *years of total policing experience* (0 = none; 1 = less than 1 year; 2 = 1–2; 3 = 3–5; 4 = 6–9; 5 = 10–14; 6 = ≥ 15); *highest level of education* (0 = high school/GED; 1 = some college/Associate's degree; 2 = 4-year college degree; 3 = some graduate/law school work; 4 = graduate or law degree); and *city in which the officer worked* (1 = Savannah).

Block 2: Cybercrime exposure. The following direct and indirect measures of cybercrime exposure were included in the analyses. First, officers were asked whether they had read or heard stories on cybercrime in the news (1 = Yes). Second, officers were asked whether they had discussed cybercrime or computer crime recently with anyone (1 = Yes). Finally, officers were asked when was the last time that they had responded to a computer crime (cybercrime) case (0 = never; 1 = over a year ago; 2 = within last year; 3 = within last several months; 4 = within last several weeks).

Block 3: Computer training. Officers were asked two questions about the amount of computer or cybercrime investigation training that they had received. First, officers were asked how many hours of general computer training (e.g., Microsoft Word, Internet, programming) they had received within the last year. Due to limited variation, this was dichotomized into whether they had (1 = training) or had not (0 = no training) received training over the last year. Second, officers were asked how many hours of computer crime investigation training they had received (0 = no training; 1 = 8 hours or less; 2 = more than 8 hours).

Block 4: Computer proficiency. Three computer proficiency measures were included in the models. First, officers were asked how many hours they spent online for any reason in an average day (0 = less than 1 hour; 1 = 1–2; 2 = 3–4; 3 = 5–6; 4 = 6 or more hours). Second, they were asked if they had ever been able to personally use the Internet to find important information relevant to a case or to help them perform their job (1 = Yes). Finally, officers were asked to self-assess their skill level on a four-point scale: (0) I am afraid of computers and don't use them unless I absolutely have; (1) I can surf the 'net, use common software, but cannot fix my own computer; (2) I can use a variety of software and fix some computer problems I have; and (3) I can use Linux, most software, and fix most computer problems I have.

Block 5: Perceptions of the Internet and Cybercrime. Seven total items assessing their perceptions of the Internet and cybercrime were included in the analyses. Two items assessed their views of the Internet. Officers were first asked about their general attitude toward the Internet by being asked how much they agree (1 = strongly disagree to 5 = strongly agree) with, "In general, I believe that the Internet's negatives outweigh its positives." They were also asked about how the Internet has specifically impacted law enforcement. They were asked how much they agree (1 = strongly disagree to 5 = strongly agree) with, "The Internet has caused more problems for law enforcement than it has helped."

Table 3.5: Descriptive Statistics for Savannah/Charlotte Interest in Additional Basic Computer Training

	Mean	Std. Dev.	Min.	Max.	n
Dependent Variable					
1) Computer training scale	0.01	0.78	-2.34	1.68	246
Block 1: Demographics					
1) Sex	0.13	0.34	0	1	260
2) Black	0.16	0.37	0	1	253
3) Other race	0.09	0.29	0	1	253
4) Age	36.88	8.69	22	63	256
5) Years in policing	4.18	1.62	1	6	263
6) Education	1.52	0.94	0	4	262
7) Site	0.53	0.50	0	1	263
Block 2: Cybercrime Exposure					
1) News	0.80	0.40	0	1	251
2) Discussion	0.19	0.39	0	1	261
3) Cybercase	0.76	1.16	0	4	257
Block 3: Training					
1) Computer training	0.28	0.45	0	1	257
2) Cyber investigation training	0.17	0.51	0	2	263
Block 4: Computer Proficiency					
1) Hours online	0.84	0.99	0	4	263
2) Internet case	0.67	0.47	0	1	253
3) Computer skill	1.56	0.65	0	3	263
Block 5: Perceptions of Internet and Cybercrime					
1) Internet positives	2.35	0.97	1	5	252
2) Internet/impact LE	2.53	0.96	1	5	253
3) Uniqueness	3.18	0.85	1	5	251
4) Frequency	3.81	0.93	1.14	5	253
5) Seriousness	4.15	0.61	1.57	5	254
6) Citizens risk	2.32	0.91	1	5	252
7) Unreported	3.66	0.80	1	5	250
Responsibility					
1) Federal/state level	3.03	0.85	1	5	251
2) Local level	2.72	0.90	1	5	253
3) CCU	3.87	0.85	1	5	252

Table 3.5 *(continued)*

	Mean	Std. Dev.	Min.	Max.	n
Seriousness					
4) LE not serious	2.97	0.83	1	5	252
5) Upper management	2.93	0.61	1	5	253
Social Support					
6) Violent crime recognition	3.08	0.95	1	5	253
7) Traditional crime recognition	3.17	0.90	1	5	252
Value of cybercrime investigations					
8) Drains valuable resources	2.34	0.92	1	5	252
9) Computer stakeouts	3.42	0.92	1	5	252
Impact on policing					
10) Dramatically change	3.56	0.82	2	5	254

Five items assessing their perceptions of cybercrime were included. These included their perceptions of the uniqueness, frequency, and seriousness of cybercrime, as well as their perceptions of whether citizens understand the risk of cybercrime and whether they report it. Uniqueness was measured by an item asking how much they agree (1 = strongly disagree to 5 = strongly agree) with: "Cybercrime is mostly traditional crimes using a computer." Frequency of cybercrime was measured by averaging their responses to how frequently (1 = never to 5 = very frequently) they perceived seven different computer crimes occurred: copyright infringement such as software and media piracy; credit card fraud; electronic theft of money from accounts; online harassment; identity theft; pedophilia on the Internet; and viruses and malicious software infection. The five measures created a highly reliable scale ($\alpha = .93$). The seriousness of cybercrime scale was created by averaging the responses to how serious (1 = least serious to 5 = most serious) the same seven cybercrimes listed above were based on the financial and emotional harm to victims, and their threat to life, liberty, and personal property ($\alpha = .85$). Finally, the officers were asked two questions on their perceptions of how citizens have responded to cybercrime. Officers were asked whether they agreed (1 = strongly disagree to 5 = strongly agree) with, "Citizens in our community understand the risk of computer crime." In addition, they were asked whether they agreed whether most computer crimes go unreported to law enforcement.

Block 6: Views on Policing Cybercrime. Ten items that assessed the officers' views on policing cybercrime were grouped into five categories: (1) responsibility for responding to local computer crimes; (2) seriousness of police response; (3) social support; (4) value of cybercrime investigations; and (5) impact on policing. Three questions were asked to ascertain who they thought should be responsible for handling local cybercrime. They were asked whether they agreed (1 = strongly disagree to 5 = strongly agree) that: (1) the federal and state governments were primarily responsible ("Controlling computer crime in the local area is the primary responsibility of the federal government."); (2) local law enforcement agencies were primarily responsible ("Controlling computer crime in the local area is the primary responsibility of the local police."); and (3) computer crime units should directly handle cybercrime reports ("Most cybercrime reports/calls should be responded to directly by a computer crime unit.").

Officers were also asked two questions about whether they perceived that law enforcement was taking cybercrime seriously. First, they were asked whether they agreed (1 = strongly disagree to 5 = strongly agree) that, "Computer crime is not taken seriously enough by law enforcement." Second, a scale measuring officer perceptions of upper management response to cybercrime was created by averaging the responses to two items: "Upper management in our department treats cybercrime serious enough" and "Upper management in our department is taking the proper steps to address cybercrime" ($\alpha = .70$). For social support, officers were asked both whether they think that investigating violent crime in comparison to other crimes should receive more recognition and whether they think that an officer catching a traditional criminal would actually receive more recognition than the catching of a computer criminal.

Finally, officers were asked two questions on the value of cybercrime investigations and one question on how cybercrime would affect the future of policing. Regarding the perceived value of cybercrime investigations, officers were asked whether they agreed (1 = strongly disagree to 5 = strongly agree) with two items: "Investigating cybercrime drains valuable police resources that should be spent investigating other crimes" and "Conducting a stakeout on the computer is just as important as a traditional stakeout." To assess the impact of cybercrime on policing, officers were asked whether they agreed with, "Cybercrime will dramatically change police work."

We examined the predictors of officer interest in basic computer training by running hierarchical ordinary least squares models using pairwise deletion.[4]

---

4. Hierarchical ordinary least squares regression allows us to examine the effect of each independent measure on the dependent variable while controlling for the effects of the other independent measures, similar to ordinary least squares regression. In Hierarchical modeling, categories of variables are entered as groups into the models in order to be able to examine the impact of the category of variables on the amount of variation explained in the dependent variable.

Blocks of predictors were entered into the models from most distant, starting with demographics, to the more proximate predictors, such as current computer skills and perceptions. Table 3.6 contains the findings of the hierarchical ordinary least squares models predicting officer interest in additional basic computer training. In these models, the following blocks significantly improved the models: Model 1: demographics ($\Delta F = 6.793$); Model 5: perceptions of the Internet and cybercrime ($\Delta F = 2.768$); and Model 6: views on policing cybercrime ($\Delta F = 4.870$). Thus, officers' overall perceptions of how law enforcement has responded to cybercrime significantly influences both their interest in basic computer training (see Table 3.6 for detail) and cyber investigation training (Holt & Bossler, 2012b). Perceptions of the Internet and cybercrime may affect overall whether officers are interested in additional basic computer training (Table 3.6), but not more advanced cyber investigation training (Holt & Bossler, 2012b). Officers' computer proficiency levels were overall related to whether they were interested in cyber investigation training (Holt & Bossler, 2012b), but not basic computer training (Table 3.6).

Model 1 indicates that of the demographic measures, officers who were neither White nor Black (other race), older, and work in Savannah were more interested in basic computer training than White and Black officers as well as their younger colleagues. These results were congruent with the same type of officers who were more interested in receiving cyber investigation training (Holt & Bossler, 2012b). These results are consistent through models 2–6 with the exception that *other race* loses its statistical significance in later models. Thus, older officers and those in Savannah still showed interest in additional basic computer training even after controlling for exposure, past training, their current levels of computer proficiency, and their perceptions on a wide variety of issues regarding cybercrime and the police response.

Model 2 illustrates that no measure within this block significantly influenced officer interest in basic computer training. These findings in this current analysis are consistent with prior research on officer interest in cybercrime training (Holt & Bossler, 2012b). Model 3 indicates that past computer or cyber investigation training did not significantly influence the officers' interest in basic computer training.

Model 4 indicates that the computer proficiency as a whole significantly influenced officers' interest in basic computer training, but that no specific measure was statistically significant at the 95 percent confidence level. It may appear that officers who spend more time online were interested in additional basic computer training. This effect was not present in models 5 and 6, which is quite different from prior research, which found a relationship between computer proficiency and interest in cybercrime training (Holt & Bossler, 2012b). Officers with higher levels of computer skills were still more interested in advanced cyber investigation training even after controlling for a wide variety of factors. Although officers who use the Internet more and have higher levels of computer skills were more interested in cyber investigation training, it is interesting that officers who do not use the Internet and who have less computer proficiency were not more interested in basic computer training. Thus, officers who were interested in technology were interested in learning more advanced cyber investigation skills; officers who were not interested in technology and have little computer skills, however, were not even interested in improving their capacity through basic computer training.

Table 3.6: Hierarchical OLS Models Predicting Officer Interest in More Computer Training (n=246)

	Zero-order	Model 1	Model 2	Model 3	Model 4	Model 5	Model 6
Block 1: Demographics							
Sex	-0.004	0.064	0.056	0.057	0.075	0.069	0.059
Race	0.135*	0.088	0.088	0.086	0.076	0.099	0.061
Other race	0.098	0.121*	0.122	0.118#	0.104#	0.097	0.052
Age	0.132*	0.282**	0.290***	0.298***	0.308***	0.277**	0.226**
Years policing	-0.033	-0.023	-0.040	-0.053	-0.051	-0.008	0.026
Education	-0.170**	-0.010	-0.022	-0.028	-0.048	-0.033	-0.045
Site (Savannah = 1)		0.303**	0.251***	0.228**	0.231**	0.228**	0.216**	0.170*
Block 2: Cybercrime exposure							
News	0.089	--	0.102#	0.095	0.071	0.058	0.036
Discussion	0.029	--	0.079	0.069	0.036	0.026	0.058
Cybercase	-0.023	--	-0.034	-0.034	-0.049	-0.068	-0.092
Block 3: Training							
Computer training	-0.008	--	--	-0.052	-0.051	-0.020	-0.041
Cyber investigation training	-0.080	--	--	0.055	0.038	0.027	0.001
Block 4: Computer proficiency							
Hours online	0.094	--	--	--	0.107#	0.071	0.047
Internet case	-0.020	--	--	--	0.074	0.008	-0.016
Computer skill	-0.015	--	--	--	0.072	0.064	0.031

Table 3.6 *(continued)*

	Zero-order	Model 1	Model 2	Model 3	Model 4	Model 5	Model 6
Block 5: Perceptions of cybercrime							
Internet positives	0.039	--	--	--	--	0.010	0.026
Internet/impact LE	-0.109#	--	--	--	--	-0.120#	-0.127*
Uniqueness	0.003	--	--	--	--	0.003	0.046
Frequency	0.115#	--	--	--	--	0.039	0.031
Seriousness	0.207***	--	--	--	--	0.101	0.038
Citizen risk	0.015	--	--	--	--	-0.013	0.020
Unreported	0.143*	--	--	--	--	0.200***	0.120*
Block 6: Policing cybercrime							
Federal/state level	-0.138*	--	--	--	--	--	-0.114#
Local level	0.019	--	--	--	--	--	-0.001
CCU	0.041	--	--	--	--	--	-0.065
LE not serious	-0.009	--	--	--	--	--	0.038
Upper management	0.061	--	--	--	--	--	0.020
Violent crime recognition	-0.016	--	--	--	--	--	0.027
Traditional crime recognition	0.011	--	--	--	--	--	0.070
Drains valuable resources	-0.180**	--	--	--	--	--	-0.147*
Computer stakeouts	0.235***	--	--	--	--	--	0.112#
Dramatically change	0.241***	--	--	--	--	--	0.256***
R^2		0.173	0.187	0.192	0.219	0.284	0.423
ΔR^2		0.173	0.015	0.005	0.027	0.065	0.139
ΔF		6.793***	1.368	0.693	2.495#	2.768**	4.870***

Notes: Standardized coefficients are presented; # $p < 0.100$; * $p < 0.050$; ** $p < 0.010$; *** $p < 0.001$

Block 5, which consisted of measures on perceptions of the Internet and cybercrime, added significant value to the overall model. Officers who believed that the Internet has caused more problems for law enforcement than it has helped were less interested in receiving computer training. This relationship is sensible, as those who think the Internet makes their lives harder may have no desire to either better understand these cases or spend time investigating them. In addition, officers who believed that most computer crimes go unreported to the police expressed more interest in basic computer skills. Thus, these officers may assume that cybercrimes are a serious problem, and see the inherent need to investigate these crimes.

Finally, Model 6 found four views on policing cybercrime that were possibly significantly related to interest in basic computer training. Officers who believed that the investigation of cybercrime should be dealt mostly at the federal and state levels appear to be less likely to be interested in computer training. Those who believe that cybercrime investigations drain valuable resources were also less likely interested. These findings suggest that the preconceptions of officers may be difficult to overcome. An officer who is more focused on traditional crime problems, like drugs or gang activity, may view cybercrimes as a nuisance that can be ignored (see Goodman, 1997).

In much the same way, officers who saw merit in dealing with cybercrime were more likely to express an interest in developing their skills. Specifically, respondents who value computer stakeouts were also interested in improving their computer skills, as were those who believe that cybercrime will drastically alter law enforcement. These results highlight that there are distinct officer attitudes that may impact their desire to investigate cybercrime cases. In turn, this may impact their success in the event they are ever tasked to a cybercrime case.

Summary and Conclusions

In summary, the analysis results are mixed about whether local law enforcement agencies can adequately respond to cybercrime cases. The primary response to cybercrimes takes one of two forms: specialized task forces or individual officers tasked with investigating these crimes. Though task forces may be a valuable mechanism, not all agencies have the manpower or resources needed to contribute. As a result, smaller local agencies may have limited ability to respond to cybercrimes through such structures. Budget limitations may also prevent officers from obtaining all the training needed to respond to cybercrime calls for service. In fact, there appears to be limited interest among line officers for various forms of cybercrime and computer training. Given the limitations and challenges local law enforcement may face in preparing officers to respond to cybercrimes, it is necessary to consider whether they think local law enforcement should deal with calls for service and victim complaints. These issues will be examined in depth in the next chapter to assess the perceptions of line officers and investigators.

Chapter 4

Police Officer Attitudes toward the Law Enforcement Response to Cybercrime

The prior chapters demonstrate that there is variation in local law enforcement's response to cybercrime. Though cybercrimes may be underreported (Hinduja, 2004; Holt, 2003; Holt et al., 2010; Stambaugh et al., 2001; Taylor et al., 2010; Wall, 2001, 2007), local law enforcement is not entirely disconnected from these offenses. Officers appear to recognize the frequency and severity of certain forms of cybercrime, despite potentially limited reporting. In addition, there is some interest among local officers to receive training to investigate cybercrime cases and general computer skill development. There are, however, certain demographic and attitudinal factors that are associated with officer interest in training, which may affect their success in the field.

In light of these findings, there is also substantive value in understanding how officers think they should deal with these crimes from both a tactical and strategic perspective (Bossler & Holt, 2012). Many scholars and pundits have argued that local law enforcement should engage more directly with all the entities involved in policing cyberspace (see Chapter 1 for a breakdown). The development of any program to coordinate law enforcement with citizens, industry, and other community groups requires buy-in from officers in order to ensure success (e.g., Skogan & Hartnett, 1997). If officers do not support these programs or believe in their utility, then they may not be implemented properly or could break down over time.

Thus, there is a need to understand how officers perceive the value of various strategies to combat cybercrime that have been recommended by practitioners and the research community. This chapter will begin by examining officer perceptions of the ways that cybercrime cases are supported within their agencies. Then, the factors associated with officer support for working with citizens in the community are assessed using data from police officers in two cities.

Perceptions of Traditional Strategies to Combat Cybercrime

Police scholars and administrators have called on local law enforcement to respond to cybercrime, primarily by improving response capabilities for cybercrime calls for service (e.g., Stambaugh et al., 2001). Many of these recommendations have focused on additional computer training for front line officers (Brenner, 2008; Goodman, 1997; Hinduja, 2007; Holt et al., 2010; McQuade, 2006; Stambaugh et al., 2001; Wall, 2007) and creating or improving local computer crime investigation units (Hinduja, 2007; Marcum et al., 2010; Stambaugh et al., 2001). Law enforcement management, rather than line officers, has made most of these recommendations. As a result, management and line officers may disagree about how first responders should respond to cybercrime calls for service.

One of the few studies to consider this issue was Bossler and Holt's (2012) study of Savannah and Charlotte police officers. They examined how line officers ranked strategies to improve cybercrime response. Each officer was asked to score fifteen survey items on each strategy's importance. These responses were derived in part from the Stambaugh et al. (2001) recommendations dealing with cybercrime, as well as recent suggestions from researchers and policy makers. The five-point scale ranged from: 1 = not important; 2 = a little important; 3 = somewhat important; 4 = important; and 5 = very important, leading to ranking in descending order (means are in parentheses):

1) Internets users being more careful on the Internet (4.18);
2) More severe penalties for cybercriminals (4.14);
3) Increased prosecutions of cybercriminals (4.08);
4) Clearer legislation against cybercrimes to increase the success of prosecution and investigation (4.04);
5) Special forensic tools and technologies (4.01);
6) Increased funding for training law enforcement agencies (4.00);
7) Creating and improving relationships with federal and state cybercrime task forces (3.99);
8) Working with service providers (e.g., AOL) to "police" the Internet (3.97);
9) Better education for the public concerning cybercrime (3.96);
10) Cooperation with the business community (high-tech industries) to improve crime reporting and investigation (3.89);
11) Structured local cybercrime units (3.80);

12) Better methods for detecting cybercrime (3.80);

13) More computer training for line officers (3.73);

14) Increased management to develop county and regional level cybercrime task forces (3.72); and

15) Working with citizens online to "police" the Internet (3.56).

These survey results provide several insights into how patrol officers think they should be addressing cybercrime. First, the lowest ranked item—working with citizens online to "police" the Internet (item 15)—received an average score of 3.56, placing it somewhere between "somewhat important" and "important." As this was the lowest-ranked score, it suggests officers do not dismiss any reasonable strategy as being insignificant or unimportant. Second, the top four ranked strategies, or responses, did not immediately engage officers but rather citizens and other criminal justice agencies. This support of changes to the legal system by these officers mirrors recommendations that have been made by scholars over the last two decades (Brenner, 2008; Burns et al., 2004; Goodman, 1997; Taylor et al., 2010; Wall, 2001). The most effective strategy in the officers' view was for citizens to be more careful while on the Internet (item 1). These findings are not much different from arguments made two decades earlier by scholars who stated that many police officers believe computer crimes result from citizens' and businesses' carelessness and that better protective measures were required (Goodman, 1997).

Educating the public about the dangers of cybercrime, however, ranked ninth in the survey. Likewise, increasing public awareness was considered one of the top 10 critical needs to address computer crime according to NIJ's "Electronic Crime Needs Assessment for State and Local Law Enforcement" (Stambaugh et al., 2001). Communicating cybercrime risks to the public may help improve recognition of victimization and foster a willingness to report victimization experiences when possible. Despite the NIJ recommendations, surveyed officers felt educating the public was not nearly as important as citizens' self-protection while online.

Officers experienced in cybercrime cases saw greater value in citizen self-monitoring online behavior than those officers with no experience. They also felt changing the legal system (e.g., creating explicit legislation), increasing prosecutions, and increasing punishments were important. Experienced officers also rated higher the increased funding for both training and specialized forensic tools. Finally, they saw creating county and regional task forces as needed to police cybercrime at the local level. As a consequence, officer exposure to cybercrime cases influenced their perceptions regarding the value of justice system changes based on what they witnessed and how they perceived the seriousness of the event.

Law enforcement administrators have also shown strong concern about their own ability, and that of the court system (e.g., prosecutors, judges), to appropriately deal with cybercrime. A common theme expressed from local law enforcement representatives is that both police management and prosecutors do not have the appropriate resources or knowledge to investigate and prosecute computer crimes (Burns et al., 2004; Hinduja, 2004; Holt et al., 2010; Stambaugh et al., 2001). This leads to a perception that cybercrime is best handled by either state or federal agencies rather than by local law enforcement (Burns et al., 2004; Goodman, 1997; Hinduja, 2004; McQuade, 2006; Stambaugh et al., 2001; Swire, 2009). For example, Burns et al.'s (2004) study of the law enforcement response to Internet fraud found that almost all participants (93 percent) believed that Internet laws, including online fraud, should be handled by federal law enforcement. Almost seventy percent (70 percent) believed that state law enforcement agencies should have a role in investigating these crimes as well. Only half (52 percent), however, believed that local law enforcement should be enforcing Internet laws. Around half (47 percent) of the respondents thought that local law enforcement were investigating these types of crime, but only 38 percent believed that federal agencies were actually enforcing Internet laws. Thus, there is some conflict between what agencies should deal with cybercrime relative to who is actually responding to calls for service.

Bossler and Holt's (2012) Savannah and Charlotte study, however, indicated the rank and file might not have as strong an opinion about who should respond to cybercrime (e.g., Burns et al., 2004; Hinduja, 2004; Stambaugh et al., 2001). For many questions, it simply seemed the average patrol officer was either ambivalent or unsure about cybercrime investigation responsibilities. For example, when asked whether federal and state law enforcement agencies had the primary responsibilities of controlling local cybercrime, half of the officers (51 percent) said that they neither agreed nor disagreed. One-quarter agreed with the statement and one-quarter disagreed. When asked whether controlling cybercrime in the local area was the primary responsibility of local law enforcement, only one-fifth (18 percent) agreed. Thus, the officers were either unsure or did not believe that local law enforcement should be held primarily responsible for dealing with local cybercrime.

Though patrol officers may be indifferent as to whether local law enforcement should respond to cybercrime calls, they have stronger opinions regarding what sort of officer should respond. Bossler and Holt (2012) found that 73 percent of officers believed cybercrime calls/reports should be responded to directly by a computer crime unit and not patrol officers. Interestingly, officers who had recent experience with a cybercrime call were less likely to believe that computer crime units should directly respond. Responding to these calls may increase officer confidence and efficacy in responding to these types of calls.

Support of Cybercrime Investigations within Police Departments

As the above sections indicate, scholars and police administrators have called for local law enforcement to address local cybercrime issues (e.g., Stambaugh et al., 2001), a call that may not be heeded by the rank and file (Bossler & Holt, 2012; Holt et al., 2010). In addition, the evidence indicates police officers are either unsure or are against local law enforcement being responsible for responding to cybercrime; they prefer computer crime units or individuals specially trained in computer crime investigations to handle the investigations (Bossler & Holt, 2012; new analyses presented in book). The question then remains, "Are cybercrime investigations valued within police agencies?"

It is unclear how the importance of computer-crime investigations has improved among local law enforcement rank and file. Traditionally, local law enforcement has placed little emphasis on computer crime investigations, unless child-pornography related (Goodman, 1997; Stambaugh et al., 2001). Often, they find that investigating cybercrime detracts from the investigation of "real" crime. In Hinduja's (2004) analysis of Michigan law enforcement agencies, he found that 36 percent of respondents reported that investigating computer crimes detracts attention from traditional crimes. In Holt et al.'s (2010) analysis of FLETC trainees, they found that almost half of the respondents (48 percent) believed that increasing the focus on cybercrimes detracts attention from traditional forms of street crime. Based on these findings, it is possible the importance of cybercrime investigations has not improved even as computer crime becomes more pervasive. If departments are feeling constrained by recent state and local budget problems, this perception could influence departmental spending on cybercrime investigations.

Bossler and Holt's (2012) study of Charlotte and Savannah police officers, however, found more cultural support within their departments than was found previously by other scholars, although some officers still demonstrated uncertainty. Two-thirds of the officers believed that cybercrime investigations did not drain valuable resources from investigations of more traditional offenses. A quarter of the officers, however, were unsure (i.e., responded "neither agree nor disagree"). In addition, almost half of the officers believed that conducting a computer stakeout was just as important as traditional stakeouts. Forty percent, however, said neither. These officers, therefore, were either positive or unsure about the value of computer investigations, but they did not display negative views of them. Whether the officers had received cybercrime investigation training was not significantly related to officer perceptions for either of these statements. Officers who had been involved with a recent cybercrime case, however, were less likely to think that cybercrime investigations drained resources from other types of investigations.

Given that patrol officers doubt whether law enforcement takes cybercrime seriously, it might seem patrol officers do not grasp how law enforcement in general responds to cybercrime, but they may have insights into how their specific departments handle computer crime. This hypothesis, however, was not supported. Bossler and Holt (2012) found that two-thirds of the officers did not know whether management in their department was taking cybercrime seriously enough. An even higher percentage—71 percent—was unsure whether management was taking the proper steps to deal with cybercrime in their areas.

In these samples, officers trained in cybercrime investigation were more likely to believe law enforcement was not taking cybercrime seriously enough. The officers' training may have led them to identify what should be occurring versus what is occurring and how little other law enforcement officers may know about cybercrime. Officers with recent cybercrime case experience were less likely to think that management was treating it seriously enough. Thus, their exposure may have shown them either less managerial support for the cybercrime investigation or the management's lack of awareness or preparedness for these offenses. This perspective might not be evident to most officers who have not yet responded to a computer crime call.

To assess NW3C trainee attitudes toward cybercrime responsibilities, they were asked to rate their agreement with the following statement: "Police agencies should have officers who specialize in computer crime." Over half (57 percent) of respondents strongly agreed with this statement; 42 percent agreed or at least slightly agreed. Respondents with more years of experience as digital evidence handlers or computer crime investigators (rho = -.190) and those who received more annual training (rho = -.136) were more likely to agree that police agencies needed specialized officers. Thus, training may have an influence on their perception of the value in having traditional patrol officers handle cybercrime calls for service

We also asked these officers receiving training whether they agreed with the following statement, "Investigating cyber crime is just as important as investigating street crime." Their responses were as follows: strongly disagree = 0.4

percent; disagree = 1.2 percent; slightly disagree = 2 percent; slightly agree = 18 percent; agree = 35 percent; and strongly agree = 44 percent. Clearly, nearly all of them (97 percent) believed investigating cybercrime was just as important as investigating street crime, or they would not have attended this training. Their support for this work keeps them working in the area. Even so, officers who have more experience handling digital evidence or investigating cybercrimes support this statement even stronger than officers with less digital evidence handling experience (r = 0.124). Officers with more years in law enforcement, however, do not support this statement as strongly with individuals with less experience (r = -0.201).

Using data from our sample of NW3C trainees, we further explored this issue by asking the respondents whether they agreed with the following statement, "My agency's administrators support cyber investigators." The responses were: strongly disagree = 5 percent; disagree = 13 percent; slightly disagree = 10 percent; slightly agree = 21 percent; agree = 35 percent; and strongly agree = 16 percent. Almost three-fourths (72 percent) indicated their administrators supported their cyber investigators with half (51 percent) responding agree or strongly agree. Seventeen percent responded that they disagreed or strongly disagreed with the statement. Officers who have received more training than others reported more support within their agency (r = 0.201) as it is possible that the trainees see the amount of training provided to the officers as a sign of administrator support and understanding of the problem. Officers in larger agencies, however, report less support from their administrators for cyber investigators (r = -0.198) as it is possible that the higher crime rates in some of these cities lead administrators to focus more on violent crime than computer crime.

As for whether cybercrime investigations will be supported by their colleagues, the evidence is mixed between a culture supporting cybercrime investigations or officers simply being uncertain. Holt and Bossler (2012) found that the largest percentage of officers—43 percent—were unsure of whether police officers who investigated violent crimes should receive more recognition. One-quarter (24 percent) agreed that they should and one-third (33 percent) disagreed that they should. Officers who had more recent computer crime experience were less likely to believe that officers who apprehend violent criminals should receive more recognition as their experience with these cases increased their awareness that these cases were not simply important but usually difficult to solve, deserving recognition. The trainees at the NW3C computer-training program were asked whether they agreed with, "The majority of people I work with support my agency's cyber investigators." Their responses were: strongly disagree = 5 percent; disagree = 9 percent; slightly disagree = 15 percent; slightly agree = 22 percent; agree = 40 percent; and strongly agree = 9 percent. A large percentage of trainees—71 percent—believed that the majority of the people they work with support the investigators. Officers who once again received more annual training reported more support from people they work with for the cyber investigators (r = 0.135).

Innovative Strategies

Law enforcement agencies have historically responded to the threat of cybercrime through traditional means. These means have included improving digital evidence collection and analysis (Brenner, 2008; Hinduja, 2007; McQuade, 2006; Stambaugh et al., 2001), conducting virtual stakeouts and stings, and reducing opportunities for crime in a situational crime prevention framework (Grabosky, 2007; Newman & Clarke, 2003; Wall & Williams, 2007).

Researchers have concluded law enforcement can reduce cybercrime by collaborating with non-law enforcement partners, an approach the policing industry often avoids. Cybercrime investigation and prevention could be improved by working with non-law enforcement agencies, entities, and citizens who already "police" (i.e., monitor) the Internet, or provide security to various extents, or both (e.g., Brenner, 2008; Hinduja, 2007; Wall, 2007). Possible collaborations include: (1) online citizens; (2) Internet service providers; (3) web-hosting companies; (4) state sponsored non-public policing agencies; and (5) other law enforcement agencies (Wall & Williams, 2007).

Internet users, or online citizens, compose the largest group of individuals who are online and have the most direct exposure to criminal activity in cyberspace. They are more adept at identifying deviance and can quickly report inappropriate behavior to authorities, Internet service providers, or both (Wall, 2001). Similarly, Internet service providers and corporate security have at least three roles in providing Internet security: (1) they maintain data, usable as evidence in investigations and prosecutions; (2) they may serve as the first point of contact for victims of a variety of cybercrimes; and (3) they can cut off Internet services to individuals in order to reduce further victimization. State-sponsored non-public policing agencies, such as Computer Emergency Response Teams (i.e., CERTs), may also be utilized as reporting resources for both public and private entities and to analyze malware to aid in protecting citizens and service providers (Holt, 2003). Also, they may be positioned to create, institute, and enforce national guidelines to protect critical infrastructure.

Expanded partnerships are needed between the private and public sectors to help facilitate the investigation and prosecution of cybercrimes. For example, the Federal Bureau of Investigation's Infragard program helps connect various law enforcement agencies with public and private organizations to identify, discuss, and address problems through various information sharing mechanisms (Taylor et al., 2010). The considerable threat to electronic critical infrastructure is another pivotal reason law enforcement must recognize the importance of working with the private sector to protect this crucial area (Brenner, 2008; Brodsky & Radvanovsky, 2011; Rege, 2013). Finally, law enforcement agencies must find support to develop increased investigation and prosecution of all cybercrime. The various role each group serves in securing the Internet and decreasing opportunities for victimization must be carefully integrated into any comprehensive plan to improve the law enforcement response to cybercrime.

One way to achieve such an effective collaborative program may be through the use of principals of community-oriented policing, which scholars and police administrators have begun to recommend (Brenner, 2008; Forss, 2010; Jones, 2007; Wall & Williams, 2007). Community policing has shaped modern police practices over the last thirty years through innovative strategies to not only identify but address local problems through community-based partnerships. Most police agencies, regardless of size, have implemented or continued to sustain some form of community policing within their city (Cordner, 1999; Skogan, 2006). The specific programs implemented vary from city to city, though the philosophy of community policing has three central components: (1) a responsibility shared by the community and police to address crime through proactive strategies and partnerships focusing on strategies other than arrest (Adams et al., 2002; Bayley, 1998; Mastrofski et al., 1995; Skogan, 2006; Skogan & Hartnett, 1997); (2) solutions to problems considered the greatest concerns of the community (Cordner, 1999; Miller, 1999); and (3) organizational changes which support partnerships in the public and private sector (Braga, 2008; McGarrell et al., 2006).

The International Association of Chiefs of Police (2009) advocated for the implementation of online community policing programs to decrease cybercrimes. In fact, scholars and police administrators see the value in strengthening existing relationships between members of law enforcement and online communities to combat various cybercrimes. Tapping relationships with online community participants may develop cybercrime-response capabilities by increasing awareness of offense prevalence and by improving reporting rates (Brenner, 2008; Jones, 2007; Wall, 2001; Wall & Williams, 2007). Engaging participants in online communities can expand the scope of police investigative resources because of their Internet knowledge, particularly in areas of the dark web or proxy-supported networks that require technical proficiency to access (Wall, 2001, 2007; Wall & Williams, 2007). This partnership, in turn, may lead to actionable intelligence to improve successful investigations and prosecutions while also increasing clearance rates of particular types of cybercrimes.

One of the greatest challenges for any initiative would be the resistance that members of online communities may have toward collaborating with police. The public considers the Internet an unregulated space somewhat removed from law enforcement oversight, particularly in the U.S. where legislative efforts toward online regulation have failed repeatedly (Brenner, 2008; Holt, 2007; Wall, 2001). Some of the most technologically sophisticated users also emphasize the value of anonymous online communications and eschew the government and police for fear that they may crack down on any behavior viewed as threatening or dangerous (Holt, 2007; Levy, 1984). Any approach to incorporating online communities into law enforcement initiatives must, therefore, consider garnering support from populations who view reporting illegal activity as snitching or selling out (Brenner, 2008; Wall, 2001; Wall & Williams, 2007). Departments may benefit from examining how community policing programs have incorporated citizens in high crime areas who had a history of mistrusting law enforcement (Skogan & Hartnett, 1998). The ability to "win the hearts and minds" of community members can increase the potential for community involvement and result in a higher likelihood of program success.

Unfortunately, few existing online community policing programs exist, aside from community outreach through social media. Also, there are no standardized platforms or frameworks for implementation based on agency size or community-identified cybercrime problems. It is unclear how such a community-oriented policing program would be structured or operate, let alone directly engage with community members. The basic framework of community-oriented policing programs deal with traditional offending and includes informational public workshops that solicit information about their concerns and possible solutions.

Along these lines, workshops could provide information to the public about cybercrime risks and what to do if an individual becomes a victim. At the same time, workshops could explain to citizens how they could serve as a witness to some aspect of cybercrime, such as the presence of child pornography on a website or threatening messages via Facebook. Also, it would prove invaluable to give citizens specific information on safety precautions they can take to reduce their chances of victimization. Concentrated effort should also be made to target youth populations for collaborative programs because they readily adopt technology and have more involvement in cybercrime as both victims and offenders (see Holt & Bossler, 2014 for review of the literature). Having more formal programs could also require law enforcement to log interactions with community members, whether in person or online, to ensure that these contacts are acknowledged and logged, but also acted upon in case of possible crime reports.

As the previous section illustrated, patrol officers in Savannah and Charlotte believed the most effective strategies to improve cybercrime response did not involve police and community partnerships. Working with citizens online to "police" the Internet ranked last out of all options. Creating strong collaborations with businesses and citizens, unfortunately, takes time. It may be viewed as complicated work and more ineffective than other approaches. Historically, patrol officers have tended to resist traditional community policing efforts because it alters their normal daily routine and mental image of "crime fighters" and instead focuses on community building and order-maintenance issues. Community policing leads directly to more contact with the public, which officers find uncomfortable and undesirable (Adams et al., 2002; Pelfrey, 2004; Skogan & Hartnett, 1997). The combined foci of working with the public and a primary concentration on order maintenance issues creates an image of "social work" to many officers (Adams et al., 2002; Miller, 1999; Reuss-Ianni, 1983; Winfree et al., 1996). Attempts at implementing online forms of community policing would add yet another problem to the already perceived problems of community policing—the inclusion of technology.

Bossler and Holt (2013) did one of the first studies that examined both the support of online community policing and the predictors that increased support for this type of initiative. Using a sample of patrol officers from Savannah and Charlotte in Spring 2008, officers were asked three questions, which ranged from general support of community policing in online settings to more specific aspects of community policing. First, the officers were asked whether they agreed (1 = strongly disagree; 2 = disagree; 3 = neutral; 4 = agree; 5 = strongly agree) with the following statement: "The principles of community policing may apply to 'virtual communities (cyberspace)' as well as they do in traditional neighborhoods." The officers were quite ambivalent about this issue (2.4 percent SD; 11.6 percent D; 48.2 percent N; 32.7 percent A; 5.2 percent SA). Half (48.2 percent) of the officers said that they neither agreed nor disagreed with this statement. Almost forty percent (37.9 percent), however, agreed or strongly agreed that the principles of community policing could be used as well in virtual settings. Thus, officers either agreed that this was possible or were unsure or had no opinion.

Second, the officers were asked to rate their agreement about actively educating the public on the risks of cybercrime: "Our police department should hold information workshops for the public informing them of the dangers of cybercrime and how to decrease their risks" (SD = 3.5 percent; D = 7.8 percent; N = 29 percent; A = 49 percent; SA = 14.3). A majority of the officers (63.3 percent) agreed or strongly agreed that their agency should intervene more in educating the public regarding cybercrime risks and prevention efforts. Twenty-nine percent, however, indicated no opinion.

The third item addressed the most central and challenging component of community policing—wanting to work with citizens directly to identify and solve problems. The officers were asked to rate on a scale of 1 to 5 (1 = not important; 2 = a little important; 3 = somewhat important; 4 = important; 5 = very important) how important it was to work with online citizens to "police" the Internet. Sixty percent (59.6 percent) believed that this was either important or very important.

Bossler and Holt (2013) further examined the predictors of officer support for online community policing within their agency and the desire to actually work with the public. They assessed the perceptual, attitudinal, and demographic characteristics associated with support for online community policing components. The strongest and most consistent predictor among officers was support for traditional community policing, suggesting that these officers valued the principles of community policing regardless of the setting. Officers who were most willing to become engaged and committed to new policing initiatives were those officers who understood both the problem being addressed and the methods of addressing it (Skogan & Hartnett, 1997). Computer proficiency, as measured by computer skill, the number of hours spent online in an average day, and whether the officer had used the Internet to help with a case, were not significantly related to any of the online community policing measures. In addition, the officers' perceptions of the Internet in general were not related to their support of online community policing.

Officers who believed that cybercrimes often go unreported to law enforcement were also logically more likely to support the basic principles of online community policing, including providing informational workshops to the public regarding the risks of cybercrime and efforts to prevent victimization (Bossler & Holt, 2013). Demographic controls, including time spent as a police officer, were not related to support for online community policing, which distinguishes itself from traditional community policing (Lurigio & Skogan, 1994; Miller, 1999; Novak et al., 2003; Paoline, Meyers, & Worden, 2000; Skogan & Hartnett, 1997). The only exception was that female officers were more likely than their male counterparts to support providing cybercrime-related informational workshops to the public.

The researchers expanded on this initial study by examining the predictors of support for online community policing, including officer perceptions of: (1) how the police respond to cybercrime; (2) how investigations were supported; and (3) how cybercrime will alter police work (Bossler & Holt, 2014). In general, officers' perceptions on how the police are responding to cybercrime were not significantly related to their views of online policing. Officers who believed that their upper management were treating cybercrime seriously enough and responding appropriately, however, were less likely to want to work with online citizens. These officers may have felt that if their agency is able to handle cybercrime cases, then there is no real value in engaging citizens. Interestingly, believing that cybercrime should be dealt with at the local level was not significantly related with support for online community policing.

Support by the officer or within the department for cybercrime investigations was not strongly related to support for online community policing or its components (Bossler & Holt, 2014). For example, officers' perceptions of how the agency recognizes catching traditional offenders in comparison to cyber criminals was not a significant predictor. Officers who believe that cybercrime investigations drain valuable resources may not believe that the principles of community policing apply to online settings. Those who felt that computer stakeouts were just as valuable as traditional stakeouts were more likely to believe that working with citizens online to police the Internet is important. Finally, officers who perceived that cybercrime was going to dramatically alter policing were more likely to support cybercrime informational workshops, but were no less likely to support the principles of online community policing or more importantly to work with citizens online.

Interest in Working with High-Tech Industries and Service Providers

Although these two studies shed light on support for online community policing, there is minimal research on officer perceptions of the usefulness of working with other groups in the community, such as businesses and Internet service providers. Scholars have argued that law enforcement needs to become more engaged with all sectors involved in "policing" the Internet (Wall, 2001, 2007), but there is a need to examine how officers perceive the importance of working with these groups. In the event that officers see no value in such endeavors, these programs may ultimately fail. Similarly, there is a need to identify the predictors that indicate why certain officers are more supportive of these innovative collaborations. Understanding officer attitudes can be invaluable to improve the selection process for specialized roles in agencies and ensure better success for innovative programs over the long term (e.g., Skogan & Hartnett, 1997).

To consider these issues, we used the same data set as Bossler and Holt (2013, 2014) consisting of Savannah and Charlotte police officers collected in 2008. Officer support for working relationships with the business community, namely high-tech industries, and service providers were treated as the dependent variables. Specifically, patrol officers were asked to rate a series of possibilities on how best to make improvements in combating computer crimes on a scale from 1 to 5 (1 = not important; 2 = a little important; 3 = somewhat important; 4 = important; 5 = very important). Although some of the options consisted of traditional strategies or citizens being more careful online, patrol officers were also provided innovative strategies. Two of these options were: (1) cooperation with the business community (i.e., high-tech industries) to improve crime reporting and investigation; and (2) working with service providers (e.g., AOL) to "police" the Internet. Overall, officers were supportive of these ideas, since the average response to both of these items was "important" (3.88 for high-tech and 3.96 for service providers; see Table 4.1 for further descriptives).

Table 4.1: Support for Collaboration with Business Community and Service Providers

	Business Community		Service Providers	
	n	%	n	%
Not important	3	1.18	3	1.18
A little important	10	3.94	16	6.30
Somewhat important	54	21.26	42	16.54
Important	135	53.15	120	47.24
Very important	52	20.47	73	28.74
Total	254	100	254	100

Almost three-fourths (73.6 percent) of officers thought it was either important (53.1 percent) or very important (20.5 percent) to cooperate with the business community to improve crime reporting and investigation. Similarly, three-fourths (75.9 percent) of the officers also thought it was important (47.2 percent) or very important (28.7 percent) to work with service providers to police the Internet. Note, however, the larger percentage of officers who thought it was very important to work with service providers in comparison to working with the business community.

To identify which officers are best suited to facilitate these collaborations, we utilized the same predictors as previous research (Bossler & Holt, 2013, 2014) to enable direct comparisons to support for community policing online. Five categories of predictors were included based on theoretical associations that should lead officers to support innovative strategies to deal with cybercrime: (1) support for traditional community policing (i.e., working with the community and non-law enforcement agencies); (2) computer proficiency; (3) perceptions of the Internet; (4) perceptions of cybercrime; and (5) various controls. The specific survey questions, scale details, and measure descriptives can be found in Table 4.2.

Support for traditional community policing (*COP scale*) was creating by standardizing the item scores and then averaging them (this measure is supported by the community policing literature: Bayley & Shearing, 1996; Pelfrey, 2004; Skogan, 2006; Skogan & Hartnett, 1997), which creates a reliable scale ($\alpha = .705$). Computer proficiency was measured through three items: (1) how many hours they spent online for any reason in an average day (*hours online*); (2) whether they had personally been able to use the Internet to find important information relevant to a case or to help them perform their job (*Internet job*); and (3) officers' self-assessment of computer skill (*computer skills*).

To measure their perceptions of the Internet, officers were asked whether they believed the Internet's negatives outweighed its positives (*Internet negatives*), as well as whether the Internet has caused more problems for law enforcement than it has helped (*Internet LE*). Perceptions of cybercrime itself were ascertained by examining the officers' perceptions of cybercrime's uniqueness (*uniqueness*), frequency (*frequency*), and severity (*seriousness*).

The officers were also asked to assess how citizens viewed the risks of cybercrime (*citizen risk*) as well as whether officers perceived that most computer crimes go unreported to law enforcement (*unreported*). Finally, following Bossler and Holt (2013), we controlled for *gender, race, years of total policing experience,* city in which the officer worked (*city*), and the officers' experiences with previous cybercrime cases (*cybercrime case*).

Table 4.2: Descriptive Statistics for First Set of Innovation Analyses

Variable	Measure	Scale	N	Mean	SD	Min	Max
Dependent							
High-tech	Please score the following items on importance of how to best make improvements in combating computer crimes: Cooperation with the business community (high-tech industries) to improve crime reporting and investigation.	1 = Not important 2 = A little important 3 = Somewhat important 4 = Important 5 = Very important	254	3.88	0.82	1	5
Service	Working with service providers (e.g., AOL) to "police" the Internet.	1 = Not important 2 = A little important 3 = Somewhat important 4 = Important 5 = Very important	254	3.96	0.90	1	5
First set of analyses							
Independent							

4 · OFFICER ATTITUDES TOWARD RESPONSE TO CYBERCRIME

Table 4.2 (*continued*)

Variable	Measure	Scale	N	Mean	SD	Min	Max
COP	Average of five items' z-scores: ($\alpha = 0.705$)	1 = SD to 5 = SA	247	-0.00	0.68	-2.30	1.61
	1) I see community policing as an important tool to decrease "traditional" crime;						
	2) Community policing takes away valuable time from real police work (reverse coded);						
	3) Community policing is more social work than real police work (reverse coded);						
	4) Police officers should try to solve non-crime problems on their beat;						
	5) Police officers should work with citizens to try and solve problems in their beat.						
Hours online	In an average day, how many hours do you spend online for any reason?	0 = less than 1 hour 1 = 1–2 hours 2 = 3–4 hours 3 = 5–6 hours 4 = more than 6 hours	263	0.84	1.00	0	4

Table 4.2 (*continued*)

Variable	Measure	Scale	N	Mean	SD	Min	Max
Use Internet	I have personally been able to use the Internet to find important information relevant to a case or to help me perform my job.	0 = No or Unsure 1 = Yes	253	0.67	0.47	0	1
Computer skill	Please indicate your skill level with computers.	Scale ranging from 0–3 (see text for specifics)	263	1.56	0.65	0	3
Internet neg.	In general, I believe that the Internet's negatives outweigh its positives.	1 = SD to 5 = SA	252	2.35	0.97	1	5
Internet LE	The Internet has caused more problems for law enforcement than it has helped.	1 = SD to 5 = SA	253	2.53	0.96	1	5
Uniqueness	Cybercrime is mostly traditional crimes using a computer.	1 = SD to 5 = SA	251	3.18	0.85	1	5
Frequency	Average score on "how FREQUENT the following crimes occur": (1) copyright infringement such as software and media piracy; (2) credit card fraud; (3) electronic theft of money from accounts; (4) online harassment; (5) identity theft; (6) pedophilia on the Internet; and (7) viruses and malicious software infection. ($\alpha = 0.93$)	1 = Rare 5 = Very Frequent	253	3.81	0.93	1	5

Table 4.2 (*continued*)

Variable	Measure	Scale	N	Mean	SD	Min	Max
Seriousness	Average score on "how SERIOUS (based on the financial and emotional harm to victims, and their threat to life, liberty, and personal property) you think the following crime types are": (1) copyright infringement such as software and media piracy; (2) credit card fraud; (3) electronic theft of money from accounts; (4) on-line harassment; (5) identity theft; (6) pedophilia on the Internet; and (7) viruses and malicious software infection. ($\alpha = 0.85$)	1 = Not serious 2 = A little serious 3 = Somewhat serious 4 = Serious 5 = Very serious	254	4.15	0.61	1	5
Citizen risk	Citizens in our community understand the risk of computer crime.	1 = SD to 5 = SA	252	2.32	0.91	1	5
Unreported	Most computer crimes often go unreported to law enforcement.	1 = SD to 5 = SA	250	3.66	0.80	1	5
Female	Sex	0 = Male 1 = Female	260	0.13	0.34	0	1
Black	Race	0 = Non-Black 1 = Black	253	0.16	0.37	0	1

Table 4.2 (continued)

Variable	Measure	Scale	N	Mean	SD	Min	Max
Years exp.	Years of total policing experience (asked as open ended question)	1 = less than 1 year 2 = 1–2 3 = 3–5 4 = 6–9 5 = 10–14 6 = ≥15	263	4.18	1.62	1	6
City	Police Department	0 = Charlotte 1 = Savannah	263	0.53	0.50	0	1
Cybercase exp.	When was the last time that you responded to a computer crime (cybercrime) case?	0 = never 1 = over year ago 2 = within last year 3 = w/in last sev. months 4 = w/in last sev. weeks	257	0.76	1.16	0	4

Second set of analyses
Police Response

Not serious enough	Computer crime is not taken seriously enough by LE.	1 = SD to 5 = SA	252	2.97	0.83	1	5

Table 4.2 (*continued*)

Variable	Measure	Scale	N	Mean	SD	Min	Max
Local responsibility	Controlling local computer crime is the responsibility of the local police.	1 = SD to 5 = SA	253	2.72	0.90	1	5
Cybercrime unit	Most cybercrime reports/calls should be responded to directly by a computer crime unit.	1 = SD to 5 = SA	252	3.87	0.85	1	5
Upper management	Average score of:	1 = SD to 5 = SA	253	2.93	0.61	1	5
	1) Upper management in our department treats cybercrime serious enough.						
	2) Upper management in our department is taking the proper steps to address cybercrime.						
Investigation support							
Drains resources	Investigating cybercrime drains valuable police resources that should be spent investigating other crime.	1 = SD to 5 = SA	252	2.34	0.92	1	5
Computer stakeout	Conducting a stakeout on the computer is just as important as a traditional stakeout.	1 = SD to 5 = SA	252	3.42	0.92	1	5
Recognition	A police officer would be given more recognition for catching a traditional criminal over a computer criminal.	1 = SD to 5 = SA	252	3.17	0.90	1	5
Impact							
Dramatically alter	Cybercrime will dramatically change police work.	1 = SD to 5 = SA	254	3.56	0.82	2	5

To further replicate the work of Bossler and Holt (2014), we examined four additional sets of predictors which might be significantly related to industry collaboration: (1) perceptions of the police response to cybercrime; (2) support for cybercrime investigations; (3) how cybercrime will impact policing; and (4) controls and significant predictors found in the first set of analyses. Following the work of Bossler and Holt (2014), four items were included in the models to assess officers' perceptions of how law enforcement was or should be responding to cybercrime: (1) whether law enforcement was not taking computer crime seriously in general (*not serious enough*); (2) whether the local police has the primary responsibility for local computer crime (*local responsibility*); (3) whether cybercrime units should directly respond to most cybercrime calls or reports (*cybercrime unit*); and (4) whether upper management was taking cybercrime seriously enough and taking the appropriate steps (*upper management*).

Three items were included in the analyses to assess cybercrime investigation support. These included their perceptions on whether cybercrime investigations drain police resources (*drains resources*), the value of computer stakeouts in comparison traditional stakeouts (*computer stakeout*), and the recognition of catching computer criminals (*recognition*). Officers were also asked whether they perceived that cybercrime would dramatically change police work (*impact*). Finally, the demographics (*sex, race*) and backgrounds (*city, years experience, cybercrime experience*) were controlled for as well as the significant predictors of cooperating with high-tech industries and working with service providers from the first set of models (*COP, frequency,* and *seriousness*).

The first step of the analyses was to look for statistically significant univariate relationships between the first set of predictors (COP, computer proficiency, perceptions of the Internet and cybercrime, and controls) and the two dependent variables. Table 4.3 indicates that the community-oriented policing (COP) scale was positively significantly correlated with both dependent variables. Spending more hours online and using the Internet for job-related tasks were both positively correlated with the belief that it was important to work with the business community. None of the three computer proficiency measures were significantly correlated with the importance of working with the business community and service providers. Rating cybercrime as more frequent and serious, but not necessarily as a unique offense, were positively correlated with both dependent variables. Experience with cybercrime cases was not significantly correlated with either dependent variable. Finally, the only significant control correlate was that Savannah officers were more likely to believe that it was important to work with these two entities.

Table 4.3: Correlation Matrix for First Set of Innovation Analyses

	1	2	3	4	5	6	7	8	9	10	11	12	13	14	15	16	17	18
1) High-tech	--																	
2) Service Prov.	0.69*	--																
3) COP	0.33*	0.23*	--															
4) Hours online	0.18*	0.12	0.15*	--														
5) Use Internet	0.13*	0.08	0.10	0.16*	--													
6) Computer skill	-0.02	-0.01	0.10	0.24*	0.17*	--												
7) Internet neg.	-0.04	0.04	-0.01	-0.16*	-0.15*	-0.08	--											
8) Internet LE	-0.11	-0.06	-0.15*	-0.13*	-0.27*	-0.11	0.39*	--										
9) Uniqueness	0.02	-0.02	-0.13*	-0.11	0.09	-0.01	-0.00	0.04	--									
10) Frequency	0.31*	0.29*	0.15*	0.12	0.15*	0.13*	0.11*	-0.06	0.12	--								
11) Seriousness	0.53*	0.47*	0.26*	0.12	0.03	-0.04	0.07	0.00	0.01	0.48*	--							
12) Citizens risk	-0.06	-0.01	-0.01	-0.12	-0.10	-0.17*	0.23*	0.11	0.02	-0.00	-0.03	--						
13) Unreported	0.09	0.02	0.01	0.12	0.17*	0.10	-0.06	-0.06	0.09	0.07	0.04	-0.13*	--					
14) Sex	0.02	0.04	0.11	-0.01	-0.05	-0.05	-0.08	0.02	0.00	0.04	0.08	-0.05	-0.02	--				
15) Black	0.04	0.02	0.20*	0.01	0.01	0.01	0.02	-0.00	0.06	0.02	0.08	0.15*	-0.11	0.09	--			
16) Years exp.	0.09	0.11	-0.18*	-0.02	0.09	-0.07	0.12	0.12	0.04	0.03	0.03	0.08	-0.03	-0.12	-0.01	--		
17) City	0.22*	0.13*	0.42*	0.07	-0.10	0.02	-0.02	-0.12	-0.05	-0.07	0.13*	-0.06	-0.01	-0.02	0.25*	-0.22*	--	
18) Cybercase	0.12	0.07	0.11	0.09	0.18*	0.09	-0.20*	0.07	0.00	-0.00	0.03	-0.12	0.17*	0.15*	-0.07	0.05	0.12	--

Note: * p ≤ 0.05

To examine the effects of these predictors while controlling for the other variables, we ran ordered logistic regression models for each of the two dependent variables due to the ordered categorical nature of the dependent measures (see Table 4.4).[1] Congruent with the findings of Bossler and Holt (2013), these two models indicated that officers who supported traditional community policing were also more likely to support working with the business community and service providers.[2] Computer proficiency and their perceptions of the Internet were not significantly correlated with either statement. Officers who felt cybercrimes occur more frequently were more likely to believe that it was important to work with service providers to address the problem. Those who believed that cybercrimes were more serious than their fellow officers were more likely to believe that it was important to work with both high-tech industries and service providers.

Table 4.5 contains the correlations between the second set of predictors based off the work of Bossler and Holt (2014) and the importance of cooperating with high-tech industries and service providers. The correlation matrix indicates that no measure within the police response category was significantly correlated with either dependent measure. Two of the three investigation support measures, *drains resources* and *stakeout*, were significantly correlated.

Officers who believe that computer investigations drain valuable resources were less likely to think that it is important to work with the business community and service providers, while those officers who saw the importance of computer stakeouts were more likely to believe that they were important. Finally, believing that cybercrime will dramatically alter police work was positively correlated with believing that it was important to work with both non-law enforcement entities.

Ordered logistic regression models were again conducted due to the ordered categorical nature of the dependent measures (see Table 4.6).[3] Officers who believed that cybercrime investigations drain valuable resources were less likely to support working with outside groups to further drain valuable resources. Furthermore, officers who saw the value of computer-based investigations were

---

1. An ordered logit model estimates the increase in the likelihood of moving up one unit in the scale of the dependent variables given a one unit change in the independent variable; therefore, significant coefficients indicate a change (positive or negative) in the dependent variable scales.

2. The proportional odds assumption held for both models (Model 1: X^2 64.176 (48), p = .059; Model 2: X^2 49.563 (48), p = .411). Diagnostics for multicollinearity indicated that it was not a problem as no VIF exceeded 10 and tolerance levels were above 0.2.

3. The proportional odds assumption held for both models (Model 1: X^2 54.333 (48), p = .246; Model 2: X^2 61.386 (48), p = .093). Multicollinearity was not a problem as no VIF exceeded 10 and tolerance levels were above 0.2.

more likely to want to work with outside groups to address cybercrime. Those officers who viewed cybercrime as dramatically altering law enforcement realized that they cannot address cybercrime alone, and were willing to work with outside groups. Officers who supported community-oriented policing were logically more likely to understand the importance of working with the business community but not necessarily service providers. Finally, officers who viewed cybercrime as more serious than other officers were also more willing to work with outside partners.

These models also indicate that the *upper management* scale is shown to be a significant predictor. Officers who believed that their upper management takes cybercrime seriously were less likely to want to work with the business community and service providers. Essentially, they perceived that their department and administrators are handling it appropriately and therefore have no need to bring in outside groups with which to collaborate.

In comparing these findings with previous work (Bossler & Holt, 2013, 2014), we see that some of the same predictors that affect willingness to work within community policing principles and to work directly with online citizens are similar to those that promote working with both the business community and service providers. These current findings demonstrate that officer support for community-oriented policing in the real world also influence their willingness to work with community groups, namely businesses in either the high-tech areas or those who provide Internet capabilities to individuals.

In addition, their general perceptions of the Internet and how it has impacted law enforcement is not related to officer attitudes toward external collaborators. When considering how officers view cybercrime itself, their views of how unique it is or how frequent it occurs has not impacted their views of whether law enforcement needs to work with the community. The only exception is that officers who think that cybercrimes occur more frequently thought it was more important to work with service providers. Officers who view it as more serious were more likely to believe that it is important to have informational workshops and work with online citizens, the business community, and service providers.

Considering that the models controlled for numerous beliefs and perceptions, it was not surprising that demographic characteristics were not significant predictors, with the exception that females were more likely to support informational workshops than males (Bossler & Holt, 2013). What has been surprising is that officers' experiences with cybercrime have not influenced their support of working with non-law enforcement entities, whether online citizens or the high-tech industries and service providers.

Table 4.4: Ordered Logistic Regression Models Predicting Support for Cooperation with High-Tech Industries and Service Providers

	Model 1: Cooperation w/high-tech industries		Model 2: Working with service providers	
	Estimate	SE	Estimate	SE
Community policing				
COP scale	0.633**	0.240	0.416	0.225
Computer proficiency				
Hours online	0.233	0.150	0.092	0.145
Internet job	0.420	0.336	-0.018	0.323
Skill level	-0.274	0.227	-0.160	0.218
Perceptions of Internet				
Internet negatives	-0.046	0.169	0.006	0.163
Internet LE	-0.223	0.166	-0.104	0.160
Perceptions of Cybercrime				
Uniqueness	0.106	0.167	-0.084	0.161
Frequency	0.246	0.189	0.372*	0.180
Seriousness	1.827**	0.319	1.361***	0.292
Citizens risk	-0.091	0.170	0.042	0.163
Unreported LE	0.299	0.187	0.148	0.178
Controls				
Female	-0.177	0.417	-0.232	0.406
Black	-0.067	0.410	-0.298	0.397
Yrs. Policing	0.101	0.091	0.087	0.088
City	0.224	0.335	0.068	0.315
Cybercrime case	0.028	0.127	-0.017	0.123
-2LL	395.741		458.756	
X^2 (16)	98.415	**	64.736	**
Nagelkerke R^2	0.409		0.286	
N	214		214	

Notes: Standardized coefficients are presented; # p < 0.100; * p < 0.050; ** p < 0.010; *** p < 0.001

Table 4.5: Correlation Matrix for Second Set of Innovation Analyses

	1	2	3	4	5	6	7	8	9	10	11	12	13	14	15	16	17
1) High-tech	--																
2) Service prov.	0.69*	--															
3) Not serious	0.01	-0.09	--														
4) Local resp.	0.03	-0.05	-0.06	--													
5) Cyber unit	0.09	0.08	0.02	0.00	--												
6) Upper mgmt.	-0.12	-0.07	-0.29*	0.13*	0.14*	--											
7) Drain resource	-0.29*	-0.26*	0.01	-0.08	0.01	0.20*	--										
8) Stakeout	0.31*	0.24*	-0.05	0.31*	0.03	0.15*	-0.21*	--									
9) Recognition	-0.10	-0.03	0.14*	-0.04	0.07	-0.02	0.07	-0.12	--								
10) Dramatic	0.23*	0.28*	0.13*	-0.02	0.25*	-0.05	-0.12	0.29*	0.05	--							
11) COP	0.33*	0.23*	-0.15*	0.11	-0.10	0.13*	-0.31*	0.35*	-0.01	0.13*	--						
12) Frequency	0.31*	0.29*	0.03	0.02	0.07	0.01	-0.10	0.12	-0.02	0.02	0.15*	--					
13) Seriousness	0.53*	0.47*	-0.10	0.04	0.05	0.12	-0.18*	0.29*	-0.19*	0.10	0.26*	0.48*	--				
14) Female	0.02	0.04	-0.01	-0.19*	-0.16*	-0.12	-0.01	0.08	0.03	-0.03	0.11	0.04	0.08	--			
15) Black	0.04	0.02	-0.27*	0.02	-0.14*	0.14*	-0.07	0.14*	-0.17*	0.01	0.20*	0.02	0.08	0.09	--		
16) Yrs. Exp.	0.09	0.11	-0.03	0.10	0.03	0.00	0.07	0.06	-0.08	-0.05	-0.18*	0.03	0.03	-0.12	-0.01	--	
17) City	0.22*	0.13*	-0.11	-0.10	-0.12	-0.08	-0.14*	0.10	-0.03	0.09	0.42*	-0.07	0.13*	-0.02	0.25*	-0.22*	--
18) Cybercrime	0.12	0.07	0.06	-0.02	-0.17*	-0.18*	-0.13*	0.07	0.08	-0.07	0.11	-0.00	0.03	0.15*	-0.07	0.05	0.12

Note: * p ≤ 0.05

Table 4.6: Ordered Logistic Regression Models — Innovation — Second Set of Variables

	Model 1: Cooperation w/high-tech industries		Model 2: Working with service providers	
	Estimate	SE	Estimate	SE
Police response				
Not serious enough	0.038	0.203	-0.273	0.196
Local responsibility	-0.124	0.184	-0.264	0.176
Cybercrime unit	0.249	0.178	0.119	0.171
Upper management	-1.082**	0.295	-0.589*	0.277
Investigation support				
Drains resources	-0.414*	0.180	-0.438*	0.172
Computer stakeout	0.361#	0.192	0.173	0.180
Recognition	0.023	0.171	0.152	0.163
Impact on policing				
Dramatically alter	0.412*	0.196	0.647**	0.191
Controls				
COP	0.603*	0.268	0.296	0.251
Frequency	0.286	0.186	0.303#	0.176
Seriousness	1.832**	0.334	1.470**	0.306
Demographics				
Female	-0.420	0.444	-0.301	0.433
Black	-0.043	0.431	-0.330	0.413
Years experience	0.073	0.095	0.125	0.090
City	0.151	0.352	0.046	0.330
Cybercrime exp.	0.133	0.130	0.006	0.123
-2LL	370.936		428.105	
χ^2 (16)	129.173 **		102.105 **	
Nagelkerke R^2	0.501		0.412	
N	215		216	

Notes: # $p < 0.100$; * $p < 0.050$; ** $p < 0.010$; *** $p < 0.001$

Considering the importance that scholars have placed on law enforcement working with non-law enforcement agencies to better address various forms of cybercrime, police administrators need to be better prepared to identify those officers who will be best able to work on these collaborations. These findings coupled with the work of Bossler and Holt (2013, 2014) have consistently found that computer proficiency and skill, at least how it has been measured in these studies, is not related to believing that it is important to work with any non-law enforcement entity on this topic. In addition, having previous case experience did not also impact whether officers thought it important to improve these collaborations. Finally, demographic characteristics were not relevant as well once appropriate controls were examined.

Thus, police administrators should not assume that selecting officers with specific technical proficiencies would be best for cybercrime-oriented community programs. This may seem sensible at the outset as such officers may have the skills and knowledge to communicate these problems to others and perform certain tasks. Departments would want to use the resources that they already have rather than train someone new for these roles. Instead, decision-makers should focus on officers who appreciate working with the public and demonstrate the effort to build lasting partnerships.

In addition, officers who are identified for these collaborations need to understand the seriousness of cybercrime, the unique investigative techniques that must be employed, and the general impact this will have on policing generally. Such officers may not, however, be technologically-oriented and will require training to be brought up to speed (FLETC, 2012; NIJ, 2008; NW3C, 2012). The budgetary constraints experienced, particularly at the local level, may lead administrators to select officers on the basis of technological proficiency rather than their desire to engage in community policing or their capacity for community engagement. The results from this research indicate that it would be more advantageous to select officers who are already supportive of such an initiative as they may be more effective once trained, rather than an officer who is disengaged at the outset.

There is also a clear need for research on the ways that citizens view their role in policing cybercrimes, as well as the willingness of businesses and service providers to collaborate with law enforcement in various ways. It is unknown how many collaborations exist between industry and local law enforcement, let alone how they are structured, their perceived efficacy, and how they may be improved. Thorough implementation and evaluation research of these programs and collaborations is thus essential for the next wave of efforts with agencies across the U.S. These studies should not only be empirically driven, but also focus on in-depth interviews of officers to gather a more nuanced understanding of how they perceive these issues and what they think should be done. Only after this type of research is conducted will we have a better understanding of proven strategies that can help us better address these crimes.

Summary and Conclusions

As technology continues to become intertwined into every facet of society, it will continue to play a larger role in the commission of crime. In response to these perceived threats, local law enforcement has been asked to become more engaged. Patrol officers are thus being asked to serve as more effective first responders to computer crime scenes (Hinduja, 2007; NIJ, 2008; Stambaugh et al., 2001). Scholars and law enforcement administrators have particularly argued for additional computer training and the creation of local computer crime units with better improved relationships between local, state, and federal levels.

These arguments, however, do not match the perceptions and wishes of the rank and file. A large proportion of officers were actually unsure about what they thought about cybercrime and what should be done about it. Most of the officers had little direct experience with computer crime to help them form opinions on these offenses. The evidence seems rather clear, however, that officers would prefer to not become directly involved in cybercrime cases and would rather see changes in citizen online behavior and to the legal system. These perceptions need to be taken into consideration when trying to engage local law enforcement into a comprehensive strategy to address various forms of cybercrime. Finally, innovative strategies consisting of working with online entities, including citizens, high-tech industries, and service providers, need to be continued to be focused upon by selecting officers who approve of these new strategies. The implications for how such programs or policy initiatives should be developed will be explored in Chapter 6.

Chapter 5

Stress, Strain, and Satisfaction among Cybercrime Investigators

Police work varies in its day-to-day tasks: rescuing lost children, citing speeding motorists, writing reports, testifying in court, moderating domestic disputes, and merely patrolling a beat. Most of these activities involve "street crimes" where the victim and offender have physically interacted through violence or property theft. These interactions produce physical evidence at the scene, which can include footprints, blood, hair, fingerprints, and DNA from both the victim and offender.

Though cybercrimes are often difficult to observe in physical space, there are bits of evidence left behind on computers, flash drives, and mobile devices. Consider an offender who sexually molests a minor and sells video of the crime on the Internet years later. The initial crime itself is corporeal, but the use of online environments to sell or distribute the video makes it a cybercrime. The unique nature of these offenses means that officers may not have all the requisite expertise necessary to detect, collect, and process a cybercrime scene (see Chapter 3).

Policing street crime can be stressful because of the volatile nature of citizen interaction with officers. Cybercrime, because of its ethereal nature, should be a less stressful form of police work. The interaction with the public is limited, or virtual, and the chance of a dangerous encounter is low. Nevertheless, cybercrime poses particular stressors for officers. A few years ago, one of the authors attended a local community-wide seminar on cybercrime. The purpose of the half-day seminar was to inform educators and concerned citizens about the hazards of online activity. The seminar was hosted by a local community college and included officials from local, state, and federal agencies. In one of the breakout sessions, an officer explained a sting operation where they identified a man who preyed upon under-aged females through the Internet. When the officer had finished telling his story, he had tears in his eyes. Clearly, the process was stressful for him even in recounting the event years later. This observation demonstrated that investigating the particular kinds of stress that cybercrime investigators and digital forensic examiners face is just as important as understanding the traditional stressors that are traditionally examined.

A substantive body of research explores the occupational reactions of line officers in policing agencies working traditional street crimes (Dowler, 2005; Haarr & Morash, 1999; Morash, Haarr, & Kwak, 2006); however, few studies have focused on the stress and satisfaction reported by cybercrime investigators working in specialized positions within law enforcement agencies. Thus, this chapter explores the prevalence of job stress and satisfaction among a population of investigators who completed digital forensic investigation training provided by the National White Collar Crime Center. The coping mechanisms employed by investigators outside of the office are also detailed, including the use of mental health services. Using a second set of data provided by investigators undergoing NW3C training, we also measured the prevalence of trauma and secondary stress reported by cybercrime examiners. The findings help to illuminate the distinct impact that investigations have on the individuals working cases and consider their mental health needs generally.

Job Stress in Policing

Occupational Experiences in Law Enforcement

A substantive body of research on law enforcement officers' reactions to their working conditions identifies circumstances that increase work stress. High levels of stress can lead to employee absenteeism, high turnover, and low productivity. Thus, agencies want to identify these stressors to optimize employee effectiveness. In addition, these issues are especially troubling for criminal justice agencies due to the resources required to hire and train new individuals if officers leave the agency (Anshel, 2000; Maslach, 2003; Van Yperen & Snijders, 2000).

Work stress can also increase hostility between officers and residents during calls for service, which may affect public cynicism and distrust of the agency. Under such circumstances, citizens are more likely to sue individual officers or agencies (Tang & Hammontree, 1992). The inherent dangers in policing likewise produce stress during citizen encounters because officers may face significant physical harm from suspects. In addition, officers may witness a variety of brutal or violent crimes in the course of their jobs (Dowler, 2005; He et al., 2002).

Research on law enforcement officers' work stress indicates it is high for several reasons. For example, fundamental role conflicts, measured through competing job demands and different or unclear standards for completing specific tasks, may significantly increase stress on a daily basis (Cullen et al., 1985;

Pogrebin, 1978). Also, a lack of clear conduct guidelines for work tasks, called role ambiguity, decreases employee job satisfaction (Coman & Evans, 1991; He et al., 2002; Symonds, 1970). Organizational factors, such as insufficient training, lack of supervisory support for decision-making, and the inability to affect workplace policies or procedures, may also increase overall job stress (Coman & Evans, 1991; He et al., 2002; Symonds, 1970). Agency size has also shown to be a relevant factor as officers working in large cities report higher levels of stress than officers in smaller jurisdictions (Brooks & Piquero, 1998; Crank & Caldero, 1991; Oliver & Meier, 2004). The impact of agency size, however, may reflect variations in managerial structures, physical danger, and role conflicts across different agencies.

High work stress is also correlated with low job satisfaction as measured through personal fulfillment or enjoyment (Belknap & Shelly, 1992; Carlan, 2007; Dantzker, 1994; Krimmel & Gormley, 2003). Individual stress and job dissatisfaction similarly affect the satisfaction within the organization by increasing aggression or hostility toward fellow employees (Morgan et al., 2005; Tang & Hammontree, 1992). Conversely, support from fellow officers, rather than friends and family, reduces stress because colleagues better understand the unique nature of policing (Graf, 1986; LaRocco, House, & French, 1980; Morash et al., 2006).

Cybercrime, Forensic Investigation, and Stress

With these conditions for policing in mind, it is reasonable to expect cybercrime examiners would similarly report high stress because of both the inherent stress in policing, as discussed above, and the various complexities related to the nature of computer-related crime and the dynamics of forensic investigation. In addition, cases involving digital evidence require specialized technologies to search and seize data. Examiners need unique equipment to capture bit-for-bit images of a hard drive, cell phone, or memory stick to search the device as it existed at the time of seizure (Britz, 2010; Ferraro & Casey, 2005; Hagy, 2007). Examiners also utilize specialized software programs, such as Encase or the ForensicToolKit (FTK), to examine the image to determine file locations and contents, Internet search histories, and other materials (Britz, 2010).

The material costs to establish a lab, however, are very prohibitive for local agencies that must operate within existing limited budgets (Britz, 2010; Stambaugh et al., 2010). For instance, a one-year site license and maintenance fee for Encase is $3,600 while FTK is $5,200 (Mizota, 2013). This does not include the costs for the computer equipment needed to install this software for use in analysis or all the necessary peripheral equipment required to seize forensic images of hard drives and mobile phones (Ferraro & Casey, 2005).

The costs for training and staffing a cybercrime and digital forensic unit may also hinder the investigative capabilities of the local agencies (Ferraro & Casey, 2005; Senjo, 2004). A one-year training program for EnCase software costs $5,500 per person. This does not include the costs for any certifications that indicate the users' mastery of the program (EnCase, 2014). In addition, these courses must be taken at EnCase facilities, which are only present in four sites across the United States. Travel costs are also not included in this price. As a result, budgetary constraints may significantly diminish the capacity of local law enforcement agencies to staff and develop a lab to properly handle digital evidence. These conditions may cause added stress for digital forensic examiners who are asked to properly investigate various forms of cybercrime.

The jurisdictional and investigative difficulties that arise in the course of investigations may hinder prosecutions as well (Britz, 2010; Wall, 2007). For instance, if an unknown offender used financial information stolen from a local victim to acquire hundreds of dollars, the police may be unable to persuade the prosecutor to take the case (Peretti, 2009). These issues may explain why so few hacking cases are investigated at the local level (Holt et al., 2010) and prosecuted at the federal level (Smith et al., 2002). As a consequence, this may reduce the likelihood of support for cybercrime investigations among management and prosecutors (see Chapter 4; Bossler & Holt, 2012; Senjo, 2004; Stambaugh et al., 2001). In fact, evidence suggests that cybercrime cases are given low priority across most agencies, unless they involve child pornography, stalking, or identity crimes (Hinduja, 2004; Holt et al., 2010; Senjo, 2004). Thus, cybercrime investigators may work in an atmosphere that does not prioritize the cases they are otherwise trained to investigate. This finding may explain why Holt and associates (2012) found that digital forensic examiners reported higher levels of job satisfaction when they had greater levels of supervisor support.

In addition, enforcement agencies' bureaucratic and militarized structure can put stress on officers (Coman & Evans, 1991; Martelli, Waters, & Martelli, 1989). When management places tight controls on officers' decision-making process, it is difficult to exercise discretion in the field (Martelli et al., 1989; Spielberger, Westberry, Grier, & Greenfield, 1981). Officers may also feel alienated by an inability to communicate their needs to management in productive ways (Golembiewski & Kim, 1990). This communication gap has particular relevance for forensic examiners whose resource needs and training requirements can strain budgets and complicate their relationship with management (Hinduja, 2004; Stambaugh et al., 2001). For example, expensive resource requests may be viewed as unnecessary, or difficult to justify given other crime problems. The failure to recognize the importance of cybercrime and digital forensics among management may also cause examiners a great deal of stress in the course of their day-to-day activities (Holt & Blevins, 2011; Holt et al., 2012; Senjo, 2004; Stambaugh et al., 2001). As a result, cybercrime examiners may feel a greater sense of role conflict as they face a limited capacity to pursue cases (Burns et al., 2008; Krause, 2009; Perez et al., 2010; Stevenson, 2007).

Research also suggests dangerous jobs like law enforcement increase stress and lower job satisfaction (Cullen et al., 1985; Cullen et al., 1989; Dowler, 2005; He et al., 2002). Digital forensic examiners may not experience physical danger on the job, though they may be exposed to emotional or psychological risks while investigating various offenses (Burns et al., 2008; Krause, 2009; Perez et al., 2010; Stevenson, 2007). Holt and colleagues (2012) found digital investigators who perceived their jobs as dangerous were more likely to experience higher stress. This relationship may be driven by exposure to child pornography and offensive or violent images that can cause psychological trauma (Burns et al., 2008; Perez et al., 2010). In fact, exposure to child pornography may increase individuals' levels of burnout and emotional fatigue in the course of their investigations. Thus, both the perceived danger of a job and the amount of exposure to child pornography may be related to higher work stress and lower job satisfaction.

The evidence is mixed regarding the ways job experiences may mitigate the relationship between work stress and satisfaction (e.g., Holt & Blevins, 2011; Holt et al., 2012). It is hypothesized that officers with more years of experience may report lower stress because they understand forensic software and evidence processing. More years on the job inoculate computer crime investigators against stressors in much the same way as experience protects against dealing with danger in traditional policing (Johnson et al., 2005; Zhao et al., 1999). At the same time, those with more years of experience with digital forensic materials may have greater exposure to harmful images, increasing burnout and secondary traumatic stress disorder (Krause, 2009; Perez et al., 2010). This experience-stress relationship among forensic examiners has mixed support. For example, one study (Holt & Blevins, 2010) found those who worked longer in law enforcement reported greater work stress, while a second study found no relationship between age or experience and both stress and satisfaction (Holt et al., 2012).

Assessing Stress, Satisfaction, and Coping Mechanisms

Considering various sources of stress that cybercrime examiners encounter, it is unclear how much satisfaction they report from their occupation (Perez et al., 2010). Furthermore, it is unclear how traditional organizational stressors, such as managerial support and workload issues, affect cybercrime examiners and the ways that they internalize and experience stress. To address these questions, we identified a sample of forensic examiners through a survey administered to a population of 1,701 law enforcement officers who completed a computer-training program through the National White Collar Crime Center (NW3C) (see Chapter 2 for details about the data collection process). Due to missing data, the final sample sizes for the models examining work stress and job satisfaction were 206 and 212 respectively. Across both populations, the respondents had more than 16 years of law enforcement experience and were primarily male, white, and married (see Table 5.1). Thus, this sample provides a purposive, yet suitable, sample of individuals working in the field of digital forensics and cybercrime to understand these vital issues (Holt & Blevins, 2011; Holt et al., 2012; Perez et al., 2010; Stevenson, 2007).

Dependent Variables

Stress. To assess the occupational experiences of respondents, a series of measures compare the characteristics of their jobs with previous research on both law enforcement and correctional officers (Blevins et al., 2007; Cullen et al., 1985). We included four measures to capture the general experiences of respondents, rather than specific aspects of their job. Respondents were presented with four statements and asked to indicate their agreement with each, using a six-item Likert scale ranging from strongly agree to strongly disagree. The statements included: (1) "I usually feel that I am under a lot of pressure when I am at work"; (2) "When I am at work, I often feel tense or uptight"; (3) "I am usually calm and at ease when I am working"; and (4) "There are a lot of aspects about my job that can make me pretty upset about things." Responses were arrayed along a six point scale from strongly agree (1) to strongly disagree (6). Each of the items was summed into a scale ($\alpha = 0.202$; see Chapter 2 for a discussion of making a scale).[1] This scale measured a general feel-

---

1. Though the alpha value indicates this is not a reliable scale, it is the most common way that stress is measured in the larger literature. For the sake of consistency and generalizability to research literature on stress and satisfaction among criminal justice system employees, we chose to retain this scale.

Table 5.1: Descriptive Statistics for NWC3 Sample

	Model 1 Stress n=206		Model 2 Satisfaction n=212			
	M	SD	M	SD	Min	Max
Dependent Variables						
Stress	15.815	2.950	---	---	9	24
Satisfaction	13.305	2.508	13.297	2.552	5	16
Work-Related Variables						
Agency Size	2.155	0.886	2.146	0.888	1	3
Experience in Years	17.000	8.234	16.850	8.334	0	38
Role Conflict	4.000	0.992	4.004	0.987	1	6
Supervisory Support	3.818	0.933	3.830	0.950	1	6
Dangerousness	3.758	0.824	3.758	0.824	1	6
Exp. with Digital Evidence	0.669	0.471	0.660	0.474	0	1
Image Exhaustion	3.332	1.322	3.327	1.309	1	6
Demographic Controls						
Age	42.310	8.665	42.220	8.659	24	65
Female	0.131	0.338	0.132	0.339	0	1
White	0.844	0.363	0.844	0.363	0	1
Married	0.791	0.407	0.783	0.413	0	1
Education	2.854	1.413	2.858	1.413	0	4

ing of work stress, providing a perspective on the amount experienced by examiners. The average level of stress reported (m = 15.815) is somewhat higher than the mean for other fields such as policing in general and correctional employees (see Table 5.1; Blevins et al., 2007; Cullen et al., 1985; Van Voorhis et al., 1991).

Satisfaction. Five Likert scale job-satisfaction measures were drawn from the Quality of Employment Survey (Quinn & Shepard, 1974), which has been successfully used in a wide range of criminal justice research (Blevins et al., 2007; Cullen et al., 1985; Van Voorhis et al., 1991). These measures included: (1) "All in all, how satisfied are you with your job?"; (2) "Knowing what you know now, if you had to decide all over again whether to take the job you now have, what would you decide?"; (3) "In general, how well would you say your job measures up to the sort of job you wanted when you took it?"; (4) "If a good friend of yours told you he (or she) was interested in working in a job like yours for your employer, what would you tell them?"; and (5) "If you were free to go into any type of job you wanted, what would your choice be?" Responses were arrayed along a six point scale from strongly agree (1) to strongly disagree (6) ($\alpha = 0.824$). This scale is designed to measure overall feelings of job satisfaction rather than specific measures of satisfaction such as particular job duties, relationships with coworkers, and salary. The mean for satisfaction is moderately high (m = 13.297), suggesting investigators are pleased with their jobs despite their experience with stress (see Table 5.1).

Independent Variables

Work-related variables. Based on previous research about the effects of work-related variables on stress and satisfaction, eight variables were included in our study. First, work satisfaction was included in the model predicting stress because stress and job satisfaction are inversely correlated (Belknap & Shelly, 1992; Carlan, 2007; Dantzker, 1994; Koslowsky, 1991; Krimmel & Gormley, 2003). Agency size was measured by asking respondents to choose from an ordinal set of responses to indicate how many officers their agency employed. These responses were further collapsed into three categories: (1) from 50 or less; (2) 51 to 250; and (3) 251 or more officers. Experience was gauged by asking how many years the respondent had worked in law enforcement. The other four work-related variables—role problems, supervisory support, perceived dangerousness of the job, and image processing exhaustion—were measured through additive indices and are discussed below.

Role conflict can increase stress and decrease satisfaction associated with any occupation, including those working in criminal justice (Coman & Evans, 1991; Cullen et al., 1985; He et al., 2002; Johnson et al., 2005). Role conflict was measured with a four-item additive scale, borrowed from Rizzo, House, and Lirtzman's (1970) research into occupational role problems. Respondents were asked how much they strongly disagreed (coded 1) to strongly agreed (6) with the following four statements: (1) "In my job, I receive incompatible requests from two or more people"; (2) "At work I receive assignments without the manpower to complete them"; (3) "I do things that are apt to be accepted by one person and not accepted by others"; and (4) "I have to do things at work that should be done differently" ($\alpha = 0.704$). The items were summed and then averaged, with higher scores representing more role problems.

Supervisory support is another work-related concept that can affect work stress and job satisfaction. High levels of supervisory support should reduce work stress and increase job satisfaction. Previous research has shown this to be the case for criminal justice employees as well (Cullen et al., 1985; Howard, Donofrio,

& Boles, 2004; Hunt & McCadden, 1985). The supervisory support measure used in this study was composed of three items designed to measure general feelings of support by supervisors (Cullen, Lutze, Link, & Wolfe, 1989). Respondents were asked how much they agreed (1 = strongly disagree to 6 = strongly agree) with the following three statements: (1) "The people I work with often have the importance of their jobs stressed to them by their supervisors"; (2) "My supervisor often encourages the people I work with if they do their job well"; and (3) "When my supervisors have a dispute with one of my fellow coworkers they usually try to handle it in a friendly way" ($\alpha = .511$).

Perceived job dangerousness was measured as an additive scale; this concept is commonly used in the literature concerning police exposure to dangerous situations while on the job (Cullen et al., 1985; Cullen et al., 1989; Dowler, 2005; He et al., 2002). Respondents were asked how much they agreed with the following five statements: (1) "I work in a dangerous job"; (2) "In my job, a person stands a good chance of getting hurt"; (3) "There is really not much chance of getting hurt at work"; (4) "My job is a lot more dangerous than other kinds of jobs"; and (5) "A lot of the people I work with get physically injured in the line of duty." Higher scores represented higher levels of perceived dangerousness ($\alpha = .450$).[2]

In addition, the models included measures regarding digital evidence handling experience and exposure to psychologically harmful materials. Respondents were asked how many years they had been a digital evidence handler (zero indicated they had not served in this capacity). This survey item was recoded into a dichotomous measure (1 = at least 1 year of digital evidence handling experience; 0 = no experience with digital evidence handling experience) due to the little variation in experience reported. Because repeated exposure to child pornography or sexually explicit materials causes emotional stress (Holt & Blevins, 2011; Perez et al., 2010), we created a two item scale measuring experiences with psychologically harmful materials by asking respondents to respond (1 = strongly disagree to 6 = strongly agree) to two statements: (1) "Working with difficult images all day is really a strain for me"; and (2) "Working with child porn images directly puts too much stress on me" ($\alpha = 0.815$). The responses were averaged with higher scores demonstrating greater strain due to exposure to child pornography.

---

2. As noted regarding the measure for stress, this is a less than reliable scale. However, it is the most common way that this is operationalized in the literature regarding dangerousness.

Demographic controls. The models included five controls for demographic characteristics: age, sex, race, whether married, and education. Age was included to understand the effect that it may have on work responses among respondents. The literature is generally mixed regarding the impact of age on job attitudes. Some studies find no significant relationship between police work reactions and age (Dowler, 2005; Storch & Panzarella, 1996), while others found younger individuals feel more work stress and less job satisfaction, which may be a consequence of different life priorities and experiences as compared to older employees (Patterson, 2003; Violanti, 1983).

The sex of the respondent (1= female) was included in the models to determine whether males and females react to their jobs differently. Some evidence suggests female criminal justice employees experience more work stress and satisfaction (Belknap & Shelly, 1992; Burke & Mikkelsen, 2005; Krimmel & Gormley, 2003; Morash et al., 2006; Zhao et al., 1999). Race was dichotomized into nonwhite (0) and white (1) due to the small number of minorities in the sample. Prior literature indicates that there are race differences in police officers' attitudes toward their occupation (Dowler, 2005; Haarr & Morash, 1999; Violanti & Aron, 1995; Zhao et al., 1999) with minorities sometimes feeling more stress and less job satisfaction than whites. Additionally, marital status was included to assess the influence of a support network outside of work on stress (He et al., 2002).

Finally, education was assessed through a single item asking respondents if they had no college, some college, a two-year degree, or a four-year degree or higher. Education appears to have a mixed impact on criminal justice employee stress. Storch and Panzarella (1996) found education is not a significant predictor of work reactions, while Cullen and associates (1985) found that higher levels of education was related to lower levels of work stress. It is plausible that officers with higher education may have better coping mechanisms to deal with stress (Cullen et al., 1985). The technical skills needed to perform effective digital forensic work may also increase job satisfaction for those with college degrees.

Exploring the Predictors of Stress and Satisfaction

The correlation matrix presented in Table 5.2 suggests that multiple factors are associated with levels of work stress. Officers who work in smaller agencies, as well as those with longer law enforcement careers, reported higher stress. Similarly, those who experienced greater role conflict, less supervisory support, perceive their jobs to be more dangerous, and lower job satisfaction were also more likely to experience stress in their jobs (Blevins et al., 2007; Coman & Evans, 1991; Cullen et al., 1985; Fairbrother & Warn, 2003; He et al., 1970; Hepburn & Albonetti, 1980; Holt & Blevins, 2011; Holt et al., 2012; Pogrebin, 1978; Symonds, 1970). Those who had greater exposure to child pornography also reported higher levels of stress (Perez et al., 2010). In addition to experience as a digital evidence handler, no demographic control was significantly related with the stress scale.

Examining the correlates of job satisfaction suggest that there are differences between the predictors of job stress and satisfaction (see Table 5.3). For job satisfaction, neither agency size nor the number of years in law enforcement were significantly related. Respondents who reported fewer role conflicts, greater supervisory support, and were married were more satisfied with their jobs (Blevins et al., 2007; Coman & Evans, 1991; Cullen et al., 1985; Fairbrother & Warn, 2003; He et al., 1970; Hepburn & Albonetti, 1980; Holt & Blevins, 2011; Holt et al., 2012; Pogrebin, 1978; Symonds, 1970). Those with less exposure to child pornography were also more satisfied with their jobs.

The correlation matrix provided enough evidence of statistically significant relationships between the measures being examined to warrant multivariate analysis. A set of linear regression models presented in Table 5.4 were conducted to assess the relationships between the predictive variables and stress and satisfaction respectively. Model 1 presents the predictors for work stress and explained 52 percent of the variance in the work stress measure.

Individuals who had longer law enforcement careers were more likely to report work stress, as did those who felt greater levels of role conflicts were present in their working environment. This is consistent with the larger research literature as these officers may have to struggle to best accomplish their tasks according to inconsistent instructions and scarce resources (Blevins et al., 2006; Cullen et al., 1985; Holt & Blevins, 2010; Johnson et al., 2005; Rizzo et al., 1970; Van Voorhis et al., 1991). Respondents who felt less supervisory support were also more likely to report levels of stress, demonstrating the importance of managerial encouragement in the course of cybercrime investigations (Goodman, 1997; Hagy, 2007; Senjo, 2004; Stambaugh et al., 2001). In addition, officers who felt that their jobs were more dangerous were more likely to report higher levels of stress in keeping with the larger literature on police stress.

Table 5.2: Correlation Matrix For Job Stress (n=206)

	1	2	3	4	5	6	7	8	9	10	11	12	13	14
1. Work Stress	1.000													
2. Agency Size	-0.127*	1.000												
3. Experience Years	0.117*	0.030	1.000											
4. Role Conflict	0.617*	-0.037	0.108	1.000										
5. Supervisory Support	-0.161*	0.154*	-0.028	-0.057	1.000									
6. Dangerousness	0.398*	-0.014	-0.089	0.335*	0.086	1.000								
7. Job Satisfaction	-0.366*	0.049	-0.048	-0.332*	0.183*	-0.133*	1.000							
8. Digital Evidence Exp.	0.107	-0.145*	0.054	-0.021	-0.078	-0.194*	-0.054	1.000						
9. Image Strain	0.435*	-0.117*	0.061	0.297*	-0.090	0.133*	-0.156*	0.216*	1.000					
10. Age	-0.033	0.075	0.803*	0.016	-0.094	-0.178*	0.035	0.066	0.039	1.000				
11. Female	-0.088	0.127*	-0.054	0.054	0.143*	0.013	0.016	0.064	-0.103*	0.028	1.000			
12. White	-0.022	-0.228*	0.003	0.003	-0.016	-0.009	-0.017	0.098	0.007	-0.062	-0.231*	1.000		
13. Married	-0.069	0.036	0.000	-0.051	-0.014	-0.171*	0.134*	0.071	0.066	0.028	-0.154*	0.044	1.000	
14. Education	-0.036	0.170*	-0.062	-0.055	0.045	0.085	0.011	0.074	-0.111*	-0.085	0.122*	-0.044	0.074	1.000

Notes: # p < 0.100; * p < 0.050; ** p < 0.010; *** p < 0.001

Table 5.3: Correlation Matrix For Job Satisfaction (n=212)

	1	2	3	4	5	6	7	8	9	10	11	12	13
1. Job Satisfaction	1.000												
2. Agency Size	0.071	1.000											
3. Experience in Years	-0.013	0.039	1.000										
4. Role Conflict	-0.334*	-0.041	0.088	1.000									
5. Supervisory Support	0.180*	0.125*	-0.006	-0.066	1.000								
6. Dangerousness	-0.111	-0.015	-0.084	0.319*	0.107	1.000							
7. Digital Evidence Exp.	-0.041	-0.129*	0.070	-0.017	-0.104	-0.208*	1.000						
8. Image Strain	-0.161*	-0.117*	0.046	0.302*	-0.095	0.132*	0.210*	1.000					
9. Age	0.029	0.076	0.797*	0.013	-0.085	-0.186*	0.076	0.033	1.000				
10. Female	0.020	0.109	-0.030	0.055	0.148*	-0.001	-0.044	-0.109	0.042	1.000			
11. White	-0.021	-0.208*	-0.019	0.002	-0.027	0.004	0.077	0.013	-0.075	-0.255*	1.000		
12. Married	0.120*	0.048	0.012	-0.050	-0.002	-0.152*	0.057	0.071	0.043	-0.166*	0.058	1.000	
13. Education	-0.001	0.160*	-0.069	-0.032	0.031	0.070	0.083	-0.099	-0.080	0.128*	-0.052	0.069	1.000

Notes: # $p < 0.100$; * $p < 0.050$; ** $p < 0.010$; *** $p < 0.001$

Table 5.4: Regression Models Predicting Work Stress and Job Satisfaction

	Model 1 (n=206) Work Stress			Model 2 (n=212) Job Satisfaction		
	b	s.e.	β	b	s.e.	β
Work-Related Variables						
Agency Size	-0.158	0.172	-0.047	0.061	0.198	0.021
Experience in Years	0.080	0.030	0.223**	-0.014	0.034	-0.045
Role Conflict	1.232	0.167	0.415***	-0.775	0.188	-0.300***
Supervisory Support	-0.332	0.161	-0.105*	0.414	0.183	0.154*
Dangerousness	0.799	0.196	0.223***	0.006	0.229	0.002
Job Satisfaction	-0.139	0.062	-0.119*	---	---	---
Exp. Digital Evidence	0.598	0.325	0.096	-0.107	0.378	-0.020
Image Exhaustion	0.484	0.119	0.217***	-0.114	0.140	-0.059
Individual Level Variables						
Age	-0.067	0.029	-0.197*	0.022	0.033	0.075
Female	-0.561	0.453	-0.064	0.154	0.532	0.020
White	-0.602	0.413	-0.074	-0.058	0.484	-0.008
Married	-0.112	0.366	-0.015	0.699	0.418	0.113
Education	0.004	0.106	0.002	-0.057	0.123	-0.031
Constant	11.484	1.802***		14.054	1.871	
Adjusted R^2	0.526			0.106		
F	18.509***			3.080***		

Notes: # $p < 0.100$; * $p < 0.050$; ** $p < 0.010$; *** $p < 0.001$

Job satisfaction was also negative and significant, suggesting those whose jobs are unfulfilling experience greater stress (Blevins et al., 2007; Coman & Evans, 1991; Cullen et al., 1985; Fairbrother & Warn, 2003; He et al., 1970; Hepburn & Albonetti, 1980; Holt & Blevins, 2011; Holt, Blevins, & Burruss, 2012; Pogrebin, 1978; Symonds, 1970). Examiners who viewed various sorts of abusive images were also likely to report stress (Burns et al., 2008; Holt et al., 2012; Krause, 2009; Perez et al., 2010; Stevenson, 2007). The emotional and psychological strain officers may experience from having to identify child pornography or offensive images throughout any given work day appear to affect their occupational experiences in a negative way.

The only significant individual factor was age, such that younger examiners were more likely to report stress. No other individual characteristics were significant predictors of stress, which is divergent from the larger literature on stress among criminal justice system employees (Belknap & Shelly, 1992; Burke & Mikkelsen, 2005; Krimmell & Gormley, 2003; Lim & Teo, 1998; Morash et al., 2006; Zhao et al., 1999).

Model 2 presents the predictors for job satisfaction that account for 10 percent of the variation in satisfaction. No individual characteristics, including age, were significant predictors of job satisfaction (Dantzker & Kubin, 1998; Zhao et al., 1999). Two of the work-related variables were significant predictors of job satisfaction. Specifically, those who report fewer role conflicts were more satisfied with their work, as were those with greater supervisory support (Cullen et al., 1985; Holt & Blevins, 2011; Hunt & McCadden, 1985; Johnson et al., 2005). These patterns are consistent with previous research on traditional policing and correctional officer roles as managerial support creates a more positive working environment overall (Babin & Boles, 1996; Cullen et al., 1985; Howard et al., 2004). Additionally, the image exhaustion scale was not significant for job satisfaction. It may be that strain from viewing images of child sexual exploitation only influence officers' levels of stress.

Coping Mechanisms Reported By Digital Forensic Investigators

Given the reported levels of work stress and satisfaction and the correlates for these experiences, we asked additional questions to understand how investigators' work affects their lives. A 16-item coping scale was used to assess the ways that investigators cope with their stresses when off the job or at home (see Table 5.5; Jackson & Maslach, 1982). The responses are presented in Table 5.5 based on the order in which they appear on the actual survey instrument. These figures generally suggest that there are a small proportion of respondents engaging in negative coping strategies such as smoking, drinking, or using recreational or prescription drugs (see Haarr & Morash, 1999; Kohan & Mazmanian, 2003; Pienaar et al., 2007).

At the same time, there are fewer respondents seeking professional help from counselors or clergy. Instead, many seem to talk to either spouses or peers about their experiences, which they may perceive as safe in discussing concerns without fear of occupational repercussions. A proportion also appears to do things to avoid thinking about their experiences, such as trying to forget about the incident or go to the movies to take their mind off of the incident. Though these may not be negative strategies, such a response may do little to aid the individual in coping with what happened. The amount of alcohol and med-

Table 5.5: Coping Mechanisms, Percentages Reported

Items	Never	Rarely	Sometimes	Often	Very Often	Always
1. I work harder than usual around the house or on the job.	7.1	17.9	42.2	19.4	11.2	2.2
2. I just try to forget about it.	3.8	12.0	36.5	25.9	15.8	6.0
3. I find some activity to take my mind off things like going to a movie.	9.0	13.2	33.5	23.7	15.4	5.3
4. I go shopping.	20.6	30.7	32.2	9.7	5.2	1.5
5. I have a drink such as beer, wine, or a cocktail.	26.9	31.3	26.9	7.8	4.9	2.2
6. I take some form of drug, such as marijuana.	99.3	0.0	0.0	0.4	0.4	0.0
7. I take a tranquilizer.	94.7	2.6	0.8	1.1	0.4	0.4
8. I take some other form of medicine.	88.3	1.9	5.7	1.5	0.4	2.3
9. I smoke more often.	86.2	4.9	5.6	1.5	1.1	0.7
10. I talk things over with my spouse or significant other.	15.7	17.6	29.6	15.4	12.7	9.0
11. I talk things over with my friends.	14.6	21.3	37.7	14.2	7.8	4.5
12. I participate in some organized groups or clubs to get social support.	46.7	21.8	21.1	5.4	2.7	2.3
13. I try to get away from everyone.	21.0	23.6	33.3	7.9	11.2	3.0
14. I engage in some religious activity.	37.5	18.4	21.0	9.0	9.4	4.9
15. I seek professional help such as a counselor.	79.8	13.9	4.1	1.1	0.7	0.4
16. I eat more or less than usual.	29.3	25.6	26.3	10.5	5.6	2.6

ication used by investigators is comparable to that of traditional law enforcement officers, as is their use of counseling services (Haarr & Morash, 1999; Kohan & Mazmanian, 2003; Pienaar et al., 2007). Though these rates are similar, there are differences in occupational roles and responsibilities (Ferarro & Casey, 2005; Perez et al., 2010).

To know what factors were related to different coping mechanisms, we regressed the individual and work-related variables, as well as the stress scale, on drinking, medication, and counseling use respectively. Each coping mechanism was converted to a binary measure (0 = no, 1 = yes) due to the limited variation in the use of medication (12.7 percent) and counseling services (20.2 percent; see Table 5.6). Though many investigators reported drinking (73.1 percent), this variable was also turned into a binary measure to allow for comparisons between the models (see Table 5.6, Model 1). In addition, the same independent variables related to job stress and satisfaction, as well as the stress scale, as presented in Table 5.6 were used to understand how they affected the coping strategies employed by investigators.

Individuals who reported higher levels of work stress were more likely to drink as a result (see Table 5.6, Model 1). Younger respondents were also more likely to turn to alcohol consumption as a result of work-related experiences. Respondents with shorter careers in law enforcement were more likely to take some medication to deal with stressful work experiences. Female officers were more likely than their male counterparts to use medication to deal with work-related issues. There were, however, no significant predictors for speaking with a professional, such as a counselor. The few significant predictors across the models suggest that the occupational factors associated with stress and satisfaction were unrelated to the use of negative coping strategies generally. As a result, it may be that riskier coping strategies may be independent of general work experience.

Exploring Trauma among Digital Forensic Investigators

Investigators reported both using negative coping strategies with some frequency and visiting professional counselors periodically. At the same time, investigators reported higher degrees of stress due to exposure to child pornography. As a result, there is a need to better understand the prevalence of psychological trauma and negative physical symptoms among forensic investigators due to the materials they work with.

Table 5.6: Binary Logistic Regression Models Predicting Coping Behaviors

	Model 1 n = 208 Alcohol Use			Model 2 n = 206 Medication			Model 3 n = 207 Counseling		
Variables	b	s.e.	Exp(B)	b	s.e.	Exp(B)	b	s.e.	Exp(B)
Work-Related Variables									
Work Stress	0.172	0.087	1.188*	0.069	0.118	1.072	-0.039	0.089	0.961
Agency Size	-0.078	0.205	0.925	-0.253	0.297	0.776	0.031	0.215	1.032
Experience in Years	0.038	0.032	1.039	-0.091	0.045	0.913*	0.008	0.035	1.009
Role Conflict	-0.004	0.223	0.996	0.217	0.321	1.243	0.018	0.236	1.018
Supervisory Support	-0.381	0.207	0.683	0.181	0.265	1.199	0.149	0.206	1.160
Dangerousness	0.024	0.236	1.024	0.171	0.336	1.186	0.147	0.256	1.159
Exp. with Digital Evidence	-0.387	0.395	0.679	-0.159	0.589	0.853	-0.143	0.413	0.866
Image Strain	-0.068	0.153	0.934	0.299	0.217	1.348	0.279	0.162	1.322
Demographic Variables									
Age	-0.068	0.031	0.935*	0.079	0.042	1.083	0.023	0.034	1.023
Female	0.352	0.553	1.421	1.436	0.652	4.205*	0.156	0.562	1.169
White	0.139	0.494	1.149	0.351	0.751	1.421	0.159	0.542	1.173
Married	-0.093	0.451	0.911	0.097	0.630	1.102	0.083	0.472	1.086
Education	0.111	0.121	1.118	0.227	0.191	1.255	0.119	0.133	1.127
Constant	2.297	2.017	9.943	-9.097	3.076	0.000**	-4.580	2.185	0.010*
Pseudo R2	0.148			0.096			0.053		

Notes: One-tailed significance tests; p < 0.05 *, p < 0.01**, p < 0.001***. Model 1: Chi-square = 2.021; -2LL = 218.117. Model 2: Chi-square = 20.894; -2LL = 123.286. Model 3: Chi-square = 16.223; -2LL=201.684

Thus, a second sample of investigators was developed through the administration of a paper survey to eight computer forensic and cybercrime training classes offered by the National White Collar Crime Center across the United States in Fall 2011. The courses were offered across the country with a total of 204 students enrolled across all the courses. Respondents were not required to complete the survey as part of the class to ensure participation was voluntary. As a result, 137 attendees completed the instrument, providing a 67.2 percent response rate. The majority of respondents were both sworn officers (n = 108; 80.5 percent) and served on a cybercrime task force (n = 75; 56 percent). Respondents also worked in law enforcement for an average of 13.86 years. Additionally, the majority were white (n = 106; 81.5 percent), male (n = 106; 80.9 percent), and married (n = 98; 74.5 percent).[3] The demographic composition of the sample is similar to that of the initial NW3C sample discussed earlier and other samples of cybercrime examiners generally (Holt & Blevins, 2011; Holt et al., 2012; Perez et al., 2010). Thus, this sample provided a purposive and convenient sample of respondents working in the field of digital forensics and cybercrime (Holt & Blevins, 2011; Holt et al., 2012; Perez et al., 2010, Stevenson, 2007).

Because many of the respondents were sworn law enforcement agents, their experiences varied in terms of the traumatic experiences they witnessed or were exposed to while on the job. In this sample, 44 individuals (34.4 percent) reported some situation that occurred in the course of their work that either disturbed them or stuck with them for longer than usual. Of those who explained the events (n = 35), the majority were real-world, such as homicides (n = 3; 7.9 percent), fatal accidents, and deaths (n = 7; 18.4 percent), or a shooting where the respondent was involved (n = 4; 10.5 percent), rather than virtual incidents (n = 19; 50 percent). These results are understandable given most respondents were sworn officers often serving as first responders to scenes of gruesome or horrific injuries and acts that may be difficult to process (Haarr & Morash, 1999; Lau, Hem, & Berg, 2006; Pienaar, Rothman, & van de Vijver, 2007; Vollrath & Torgersen, 2000; Wearing & Hart, 1996).

Eight respondents (21.1 percent) said they had trouble dealing with cybercrimes. Almost all of these cases had to deal with viewing photos or videos of child pornography in support of an investigation. Eleven respondents also said they had difficulty dealing with cases involving either child victims or child deaths by accident or harm (n = 11; 28.9 percent). Thus, there is evidence that

---

3. We do not provide a table of descriptive statistics for this sample as we do not engage in multivariate statistical analyses of the data.

some respondents reported psychological harm as a result of dealing with child-related cases (Burns et al., 2008; Krause, 2009; Perez et al., 2010; Stevenson, 2007).

In light of this finding, the respondents in the sample were asked how much they had been distressed or bothered in the past seven days by difficulties dealing with their investigative duties concerning child pornography and/or exploitation cases. Twenty-two measures were generated from the Impact of Event Scale-Revised (IES-R) survey by Weiss and Marmar (1997) to assess hyper arousal and behavioral responses that parallel Posttraumatic Stress Disorder (PTSD). Responses ranged from not at all (1) to extremely (5) in order to understand the ways that vicarious trauma stemming from an event intrudes on day-to-day activity.

Very few respondents indicated they had experienced extremely negative consequences from their exposure to child pornography (see Table 5.7 for breakdown). The most common physical problems reported were minor, including difficulty falling and staying asleep and being irritable, numb, or easily startled. Individuals also reported trying to forget about it in some way or not talk about their experience, though they reported intrusive thoughts regarding what they saw. As a result, it appears that respondents attempted to cope silently and tried to forget their issues rather than deal with them in other ways.

Secondary stress and trauma symptoms in this sample suggest investigators may feel adverse psychological consequences from their work. We therefore asked about their perceptions of the use of counseling services to expand on the findings identified earlier regarding the use of counseling. Though some agencies mandate that officers go through counseling after traumatic events or prolonged periods of exposure to harmful content, the officers may feel that it is unnecessary or provides little actual benefit. Thus we wanted to identify how forensic examiners may view the use of counseling services and any negative impact it may have on their working lives.

Most felt using counseling services would be accepted by supervisors (74.5 percent), though less seemed to feel their peers would support this decision (58.4 percent). The majority of respondents (55.5 percent) also felt that their careers would not be adversely affected by using counseling services. Despite the relative support for professional assistance, only 19 respondents (16.7 percent) utilized counseling services within this sample. Of those respondents, 64 percent felt that it was helpful as it enabled them to talk things through. A number of respondents also noted they would get advice from their friends or family regarding emotional or psychological concerns (72.9 percent). There may be a reliance on personal contacts to aid in coping with stress and strain rather than clinicians.

Bivariate correlation statistics were generated to identify any relationship between the use of professional counseling and trauma symptoms generally (see Table 5.8). The findings suggest there is no statistically significant relationship between any symptom of trauma and the use of counseling services. In fact, these findings replicate those presented earlier in the chapter utilizing a different data set. As a result, it may be that counseling services have no necessary relationship to either working experiences or behavior but may be mandated by their agency. The statistics also show that all forms of trauma were significantly and positively related to one another.

Summary and Conclusions

The findings from these two samples of investigators suggest that individuals working with digital evidence experience moderate levels of stress because of their work (Burns et al., 2008; Hagy, 2007; Holt & Blevins, 2011; Krause, 2009; Perez et al., 2010; Stevenson, 2007). They also report job satisfaction in line with that of traditional police roles and correctional officers (Eizenberg, 1975; He et al., 2006; Holt & Blevins, 2011; Johnson et al., 2005; Morash et al., 2006; Petrone & Reiser, 1985). As a result, there appear to be some points of commonality between digital evidence handlers and traditional police officers (Cullen et al., 1985; Hepburn & Albonetti, 1980; Symonds, 1970).

The regression models for both stress and satisfaction indicated investigators' experiences were influenced by role conflicts and supervisory support in keeping with research on traditional law enforcement officers (Coman & Evans, 1991; He et al., 2002; Hepburn & Albonetti, 1980; Symonds, 1970). Increased levels of role conflict, based on unclear standards for analysis or practices, were associated with higher stress, while those who report fewer conflicts have greater job satisfaction (see also Holt & Blevins, 2011; Holt et al., 2012). The same relationship was present for supervisory support, suggesting that management plays a critical role in the occupational experiences of investigators. As a result, police leaders need to increase and clarify the tasks and responsibilities of examiners and improve managerial recognition of the value of their analyses and skill sets (see Bossler & Holt, 2012; Hinduja, 2004; Holt et al., 2010; Senjo, 2004; Stambaugh et al., 2001).

Table 5.7: Response Regarding Secondary Trauma Due to Exposure to Child Pornography and Exploitation Case

Item	Not At All	A Little Bit	Moderately	Quite A Bit	Extremely
Any reminder brought back feelings about it. (n = 132)	96 (72.7%)	27 (20.55%)	8 (6.1%)	1 (.805%)	0
I had trouble staying asleep. (n = 133)	111 (83.5%)	11 (8.3%)	7 (5.3%)	3 (2.3%)	1 (0.8%)
Other things kept making me think about it. (n = 132)	103 (78.0%)	24 (18.2%)	3 (2.3%)	2 (1.5%)	0
I felt irritable and angry. (n = 132)	101 (76.5%)	26 (19.7%)	3 (2.3%)	2 (1.5%)	0
I avoided letting myself get upset when I thought about it or was reminded of it. (n = 131)	86 (65.6%)	25 (19.1%)	13 (9.9%)	5 (3.8%)	2 (1.5%)
I thought about it when I didn't mean to. (n = 132)	101 (76.5%)	19 (14.4%)	9 (6.8%)	3 (2.3%)	0
I felt as if it hadn't happened or wasn't real. (n = 132)	122 (92.4%)	8 (6.1%)	2 (1.5%)	0	0
I stayed away from reminders about it. (n = 132)	109 (82.6%)	16 (12.1%)	5 (3.8%)	2 (1.5%)	0
Pictures about it popped into my mind. (n = 132)	100 (75.8%)	24 (18.2%)	6 (4.5%)	2 (1.5%)	0
I was jumped and easily started. (n = 132)	126 (95.5%)	4 (3.0%)	2 (1.5%)	0	0
I tried not to think about it. (n = 132)	94 (71.2%)	21 (15.9%)	12 (9.1%)	3 (2.3%)	2 (1.5%)
I was aware that I still had a lot of feelings about it but didn't want to deal with them. (n = 132)	114 (86.4%)	14 (10.6%)	4 (3.0%)	0	0

Table 5.7 (continued)

Item	Not At All	A Little Bit	Moderately	Quite A Bit	Extremely
My feelings were kind of numb. (n = 129)	97 (75.2%)	20 (15.5%)	8 (6.2%)	4 (3.1%)	0
I found myself acting or feeling as though I was back at that time. (n = 129)	122 (94.6%)	6 (4.4%)	1 (0.8%)	0	0
I had trouble falling asleep. (n = 129)	108 (83.7%)	14 (10.9%)	5 (3.9%)	1 (0.8%)	1 (0.8%)
I had waves of strong feelings about it. (n = 128)	112 (87.5%)	15 (11.7%)	1 (0.8%)	0	0
I tried to remove it from my memory. (n = 129)	104 (80.6%)	14 (10.9%)	8 (6.2%)	2 (1.6%)	1 (.8%)
I had trouble concentrating. (n = 129)	112 (86.8%)	16 (12.4%)	1 (0.8%)	0	0
Reminders of it caused me to have physical reactions, such as sweating, trouble breathing, nausea, or a pounding heart. (n = 129)	126 (97.7%)	2 (1.6%)	1 (0.7%)	0	0
I had dreams about it. (n = 129)	119 (92.2%)	9 (7.0%)	1 (0.8%)	0	0
I felt watchful or on guard. (n = 129)	110 (85.3%)	11 (8.5%)	6 (4.7%)	2 (1.6%)	0
I tried not to talk about it. (n = 128)	95 (74.2%)	22 (17.2%)	5 (3.9%)	5 (3.9%)	1 (0.8%)

Reliability of Scale—alpha: .928 (n = 22)
Min=22; Max=75; Mean=27.5; n = 126

Table 5.8: Correlation Matrix for Counseling Use and Symptoms of Trauma

	1	2	3	4	5	6	7	8	9	10	11	12	13	14
1	1.000													
	114													
2	0.113	1.000												
	113	132												
3	0.089	0.680**	1.000											
	113	132	133											
4	0.043	0.636**	0.495**	1.000										
	113	132	132	132										
5	0.098	0.512**	0.499**	0.597**	1.000									
	113	132	132	132	132									
6	-0.02	0.367**	0.248**	0.322**	0.388**	1.000								
	112	131	131	131	131	131								
7	0.035	0.58**	0.573**	0.546**	0.491**	0.396**	1.000							
	113	132	132	132	132	131	132							
8	-0.12	0.173*	0.18*	0.106	0.137	0.103	0.249**	1.000						
	113	132	132	132	132	131	132	132						
9	-0.07	0.405**	0.308**	0.382**	0.368**	0.36**	0.613**	0.346**	1.000					
	113	132	132	132	132	131	132	132	132					
10	0.045	0.657**	0.46**	0.509**	0.224**	0.207	0.634**	0.256**	0.463**	1.000				
	113	132	132	132	132	131	132	132	132	132				
11	0.123	0.254**	0.172*	0.169	0.206*	0.041	0.189*	-0.06	0.219*	0.1	1.000			
	113	132	132	132	132	131	132	132	132	132	132			
12	-0.03	0.48**	0.476**	0.516**	0.467**	0.561**	0.451**	0.062	0.340**	0.433**	0.244**	1.000		
	113	132	132	132	132	131	132	132	132	132	132	132		
13	0.042	0.523**	0.401**	0.381**	0.397**	0.231**	0.392**	0.252**	0.449**	0.457**	0.498**	0.444**	1.000	
	113	132	132	132	132	131	132	132	132	132	132	132	132	
14	0.092	0.288**	0.232**	0.416**	0.452**	0.279**	0.308**	0.22*	0.318**	0.221*	0.071	0.349**	0.345**	1.000
	112	129	129	129	129	128	129	129	129	129	129	129	129	129
15	0.053	0.553**	0.546**	0.483**	0.424**	0.198**	0.487**	0.287**	0.479**	0.556**	0.239**	0.365**	0.547**	0.311**
	112	129	129	129	129	128	129	129	129	129	129	129	129	129
16	0.163	0.645**	0.773**	0.414**	0.525**	0.321**	0.601**	0.013	0.355**	0.537**	0.167	0.451**	0.373**	0.324**
	112	129	129	129	129	128	129	129	129	129	129	129	129	129
17	0.156	0.513**	0.397**	0.458**	0.48**	0.214*	0.45**	0.100	0.387**	0.488**	0.284**	0.365**	0.386**	0.456**
	111	128	128	128	128	127	128	128	128	128	128	128	128	128
18	-.020	0.476**	0.431**	0.445**	0.43**	0.244**	0.492**	0.181*	0.467**	0.47**	0.306**	0.525**	0.503**	0.495**
	112	129	129	129	129	128	129	129	129	129	129	129	129	129
19	0.131	0.525**	0.469**	0.294**	0.425**	0.243**	0.49**	0.093	0.371**	0.5**	0.274**	0.467**	0.463**	0.237**
	112	129	129	129	129	128	129	129	129	129	129	129	129	129
20	0.033	0.438**	0.397**	0.307**	0.239**	0.067	0.437**	0.182*	0.487**	0.439**	0.213*	0.211*	0.267**	0.173*
	112	129	129	129	129	128	129	129	129	129	129	129	129	129
21	0.037	0.489**	0.491**	0.35**	0.382**	0.265**	0.323**	0.082	0.308**	0.415**	0.197*	0.457**	0.400**	0.306**
	112	129	129	129	129	128	129	129	129	129	129	129	129	129
22	0.155	0.489**	0.413**	0.403**	0.411**	0.187*	0.465**	0.099	0.385**	0.498**	0.441**	0.475**	0.574**	0.301**
	112	129	129	129	129	128	129	129	129	129	129	129	129	129
23	0.037	0.516**	0.469**	0.468**	0.417**	0.46**	0.553**	0.047	0.426**	0.438**	0.351**	0.763**	0.521**	0.432**
	111	128	128	128	128	127	128	128	128	128	128	128	128	128

	15	16	17	18	19	20	21	22	23
	1.000								
	129								
	0.546**	1.000							
	129	129							
	0.550**	0.507**	1.000						
	128	128	128						
	0.494**	0.532**	0.645**	1.000					
	129	129	128	129					
	0.456**	0.589**	0.62**	0.623**	1.000				
	129	129	128	129	129				
	0.636**	0.404**	0.451**	0.49**	0.438**	1.000			
	129	129	128	129	129	129			
	0.683**	0.576**	0.531**	0.546**	0.445**	0.553**	1.000		
	129	129	128	129	129	129	129		
	0.533**	0.430**	0.579**	0.642**	0.63**	0.369**	0.529**	1.000	
	129	129	128	129	129	129	129	129	
	0.457**	0.509**	0.429**	0.641**	0.571**	0.336**	0.46**	0.588**	1.000
	128	128	127	128	128	128	128	128	128

Measures in correlation matrix:

1. Use of occupational therapy.
2. Any reminder brought back feelings about it.
3. I had trouble staying asleep.
4. Other things kept making me think about it.
5. I felt irritable and angry.
6. I avoided letting myself get upset when I thought about it or was reminded of it.
7. I thought about it when I didn't mean to.
8. I felt as if it hadn't happened or wasn't real.
9. I stayed away from reminders about it.
10. Pictures about it popped into my mind.
11. I was jumpy and easily startled.
12. I tried not to think about it.
13. I was aware that I still had a lot of feelings about it but didn't deal with them.
14. My feelings about it were kind of numb.
15. I found myself acting or feeling as though I was back at that time.
16. I had trouble falling asleep.
17. I had waves of strong feelings about it.
18. I tried to remove it from my memory.
19. I had trouble concentrating.
20. Reminders of it caused me to have physical reactions, such as sweating, trouble breathing, nausea, or a pounding heart.
21. I had dreams about it.
22. I felt watchful or on guard.
23. I tried not to talk about it.

Notes: # $p < 0.100$; * $p < 0.050$; ** $p < 0.010$; *** $p < 0.001$

We also found that demographic characteristics had limited effect on the experiences of investigators; this was also surprising, as they were significant predictors of stress and satisfaction among law enforcement in previous studies (Belknap & Shelly, 1992; Krimmel & Gormley, 2003; Morash et al., 2006; Zhao et al., 1999). Younger investigators reported higher levels of stress, which may stem from their inexperience and lack of comfort with the job (Holt & Blevins, 2011; Patterson, 2003; Violanti, 1983). Thus, scholars should further explore this relationship because the result may be an artifact of the population used in this study (see also Holt et al., 2012).

In addition, this analysis found that most forensic examiners did not engage in self-destructive coping strategies such as recreational drug use or alcohol abuse (Holt & Blevins, 2011; Perez et al., 2010). Instead, they appeared more likely to either communicate their feelings with others or distract themselves, though there was a substantial number of respondents who drank at levels often reported by law enforcement generally (Haarr & Morash, 1999; Kohan & Mazmanian, 2003; Perez et al., 2010; Pienaar et al., 2007).

There is, however, some degree of secondary trauma experienced by investigators as a result of exposure to child pornography (Burns et al., 2008; Krause, 2009; Perez et al., 2010). These levels may be somewhat similar to those reported by patrol officers after encountering accidents or harmful scenes in the field (Abdollahi, 2002), though they do not have to encounter repeatedly new scenes for hours on a daily basis. Digital forensic investigators may have to observe visual and audio evidence of sexual abuse repeatedly in support of a single case, thereby directly affecting their productivity at work and at home (Burns et al., 2008; Perez et al., 2010). In fact, exhaustion due to exposure to child pornography and offensive images was a significant predictor of work stress among this population of examiners (Burns et al., 2008; Krause, 2009; Perez et al., 2010).

Because these experiences were not correlated with the use of counseling services it is unclear how managers and law enforcement agencies protect the mental health of their investigators (Krause, 2009; Perez et al., 2010). Even though investigators felt it was acceptable to seek assistance and would not threaten their job security, they were unlikely to use counseling in favor of remaining silent about their experience. Additional research is needed to understand how these conditions affect investigators' experience of burnout and work stress generally (Holt et al., 2012; Krause, 2009; Perez et al., 2010). The policy implications and recommendations for law enforcement management will be explored in depth in Chapter 6.

Chapter 6

Implications for Policing Policy and Practice

As technology increasingly supports all facets of our daily lives, it is imperative that first responding agencies react effectively to threats and criminal activities enabled by computers and the Internet. Throughout the previous chapters, we have explored the ways state and local law enforcement perceive cybercrimes and their role in the response to these offenses. Much of this work demonstrates that local agencies recognize their role in cybercrime investigation, though it is relatively limited at this time whether by choice or by a general lack of concern among management, officer, and citizens.

As a result, many of the recommendations that can be made from this work correspond to the finding of the *Electronic Needs Assessment for State and Local Law Enforcement* published by the National Institute of Justice (Stambaugh et al., 2001) and described in Chapter 1. Though the report was based on data collected in 1999 and law enforcement has evolved since that point, there are still a variety of knowledge gaps that must be filled. As a result, we will take each of the 10 recommendations in turn and identify the implications of our findings for criminal justice policy and practice today.

Implications of Findings for CJ Policy

1) Public Awareness

Our work clearly demonstrates that while local law enforcement is cognizant of the problem of cybercrime, this may not be true for the citizens and communities they serve. There are few studies that have explored citizen awareness of cybercrime (e.g., Furnell, 2002), though it is likely that the average person may only understand these offenses to the extent that they are covered in either news media or popular culture. There may be substantive misconceptions among those in the general public as to who commits cybercrimes or the extent to which police have the ability to respond to these crimes. For instance, if the public thinks that all computer hackers are either Russian data thieves (e.g., Holt, 2013; Symantec, 2013), Chinese government spies (Mandiant, 2013), or young kids living in their parents' basements (Furnell, 2002; Schell & Dodge, 2002), then they may not think that local police can help them. Furthermore, the public, as victims, may be unable to recognize symptoms of a computer virus or signs that their devices have been compromised (e.g., Holt & Bossler, 2014).

All of these factors may make citizens hesitant to contact police in the event that they think they have been a victim of some form of cybercrime. As a result, there is a need to have local law enforcement play a role in communicating the facts about these crimes to the populations they serve. Though we noted in Chapter 4 this is not a task patrol officers view as needed or helpful, there is inherent value in engaging local police to serve as a vehicle to inform the public. Specifically, the police's credibility in communities can give greater legitimacy to the problem of cybercrime among the general public. Their ability to communicate this information to parents, guardians, and the elderly may be invaluable to help citizens recognize the inherent threats that they may face online, ranging from fraud to sexual victimization. Police often disburse information about local crime problems, such as burglary, robbery, or trespassing; they should continue to also provide tips about cybercrime awareness in the same manner.

Similarly, the use of school resource officers and in-class educational programs regarding cybercrime may be invaluable to help young people understand not only what risks are present online, but help socialize them to appropriate behavior while on the Internet. Recent research demonstrates that young people are more likely to engage in various forms of digital piracy (Business Software Alliance, 2012), which may increase their risk of exposure to malicious software and hackers (e.g., Wolfe, Higgins, & Marcum, 2008). Youth are also increasingly engaging in cyberbullying, online harassment, and sexting—sending nude or sexualized images via text messaging to others (e.g., Jones et al., 2013). While bullying behaviors may not be illegal, they can be punished by educators and school administrators (Hinduja & Patchin, 2012). In much the same way, sexting has recently been criminalized in various states and, depending on the age of the participants, can lead to the application of child pornography distribution charges against individuals who forward this content on to others (Jones et al., 2013). These acts can all be investigated at the local level, using school resource officers and public outreach specialists to communicate this information to youth populations. These efforts could help youth to recognize when they should reach out to police for assistance.

Though the Drug Abuse Resistance Education Program (or D.A.R.E.) has had little empirical support for the effectiveness of its drug awareness program, other school-based programs, like the Gang Resistance Education and Training (G.R.E.A.T), have shown success when targeting specific at-risk youth for gang involvement (e.g., Esbensen et al., 2013). Building on such an evidence-based program, a version for cyber victimization and offending can be created that uses law enforcement officers in the classroom to improve on social skills and protective online behaviors to limit cyberbullying and exposure to online sexual activities.

2) *Data Reporting*

Scholars, policy makers, and industry experts must also develop better statistical measures for cybercrime offending and victimization. As noted in Chapter 2, there is still limited evidence that citizens call local law enforcement when they experience cybercrime victimization. If a call for service leads to an investigation and arrest, that information is unlikely to appear in the Uniform Crime Report (UCR) statistics for the following year. Such information may be reported through the National Incident Based Reporting System (NIBRS), though the limited coverage across the country does not provide an adequate depiction of the total number of cases that either involve a computer or lead to an arrest. As a result, there is a need to greatly improve the ways that local law enforcement agencies document cybercrime calls for service and provide this information to the general public in an easily understood fashion. Without such information, we will continue to have inadequate cybercrime prevalence and clearance rate measures.

Similarly, the National Crime Victimization Survey (NCVS) has begun to collect data on a small number of cybercrime victimization experiences. At the moment, they have developed a supplemental survey on cyberstalking and harassment, which has some potential to capture the experiences of victims and the number of incidents experienced relative to those reported to police. The measures, however, need to be refined to avoid mis-specification of victimization incidents. For instance, the first wave of data collected in this survey had to be re-estimated as individuals who received unsolicited spam emails were initially counted as victims of online harassment (NCVS SVS, 2012). Such an error demonstrates that measuring cybercrime victimization requires careful and extremely specific questions to clearly differentiate serious offenses from less serious behavior. Furthermore, it highlights the need for improvement in the general public's understanding of cybercrime to help ensure complaints are properly directed to the appropriate agency.

One way to address both of these issues is to better integrate existing resources like the Internet Crime Complaint Center (IC3) with local law enforcement and promote its utility to the general public. Though the Internet Crime Complaint Center accepts complaints of cybercrime, individuals must first know that it exists and seek out the agency to file a report. The Center is not, however, heavily promoted by any one organization, company, or entity online. This may account for the substantive fluctuation in reports to the Center each year, as noted in Chapter 2. Developing a public awareness campaign for the IC3 may prove invaluable to increase its recognition in the general public. In turn, it could be used more effectively as a means to vet cybercrime complaints to local agency processes, while at the same time serving as an information clearinghouse. Such an idea may be imperative to help reduce the dark figure of cybercrime that has otherwise been present for the last few decades.

3) Uniform Training and Certification Courses

In general, the findings of this study demonstrate that local law enforcement has some recognition of the threat of cybercrimes, though their technical acumen and proficiency with investigation techniques is not clear. In Chapter 4, we provided evidence that officers are ambivalent about innovative ideas to address cybercrime. This attitude may stem from the perception that federal law enforcement should be primarily responsible for cybercrimes that occur even at the local levels. Of those officers who had opinions on innovative solutions to cybercrime problems, they supported community policing being applied to virtual spaces. Given this support, police administrators should identify officers who support community policing and who view cybercrime as serious rather than focusing on the computer proficiencies of the officer. Selecting an officer with computer skills might save money in the short run but could possibly lead to program failure if they do not generally support the program to which they are tasked. Thus, management should assess these attitudinal predictors in addition to the officers' computer skill levels before spending limited training resources.

In fact, it is not clear if police officers receive training or information on cybercrime case management during police academy training. Introducing these concepts early in the careers of local patrol officers may be vital to improve their recognition and awareness of cybercrime scene investigation and handling. Without an appreciation for the way such concepts are introduced, it is virtually impossible to know what training and course development is needed for patrol officers.

Furthermore, there is limited information on the total number of law enforcement officers at the local level who have received the training necessary to engage in computer forensic investigations. There is some evidence that the current population of trained digital forensic investigators, and traditional forensic scientists, are insufficient to support the current backlog of cases present at the state and local level (National Academy of Sciences, 2009). As a result, there is a need to expand the population of forensic investigators to better handle the caseload and amount of digital evidence that is acquired from modern crime scenes. As illustrated in Chapter 3, this is a challenge and requires identifying the right officers to make this transition to digital investigation and find the economic resources needed to sustain the development of local laboratories.

One of the most obvious and immediate implications is the need to enhance and expand funding for the development and training of cybercrime investigators. While this is imperative, it may be unlikely to be fulfilled due to shrinking local police budgets and increasing consolidation of service providers. One way to address this issue may be through needs assessment and direct engagement with the various entities that offer digital forensic investigation training to law enforcement, such as the National White Collar Crime Center. Since these agencies directly engage with both new and trained investigators, they have immediate access to investigators who can give a better sense of the scope of the problem of cybercrime at the local level. Additionally, these investigators can communicate the challenges they are dealing with in terms of equipment, certifications, and skill building needed to better investigate the issues that are viewed as most critical by their agency. This sort of research could serve as an initial foray into the state of digital forensic investigations at the state and local level, and provide invaluable information on both the quality of training and preparation for forensic investigators, and identify new tools or resources that may automate portions of their jobs and reduce the workload that must be directly dealt with by otherwise overworked investigators.

4) *Onsite Management Assistance for Electronic Crime Units and Task Forces*

Our findings demonstrate that officers perceive dedicated cybercrime task forces as a valuable resource. The availability of these resources may, however, be extremely limited based on funding and local staff with sufficient cybercrime training. Many of the arrests made for child pornography cases are generated by task forces, such as Internet Crimes Against Children (ICAC) task forces (see Chapter 3), and appear to have some demonstrable impact on cybercrime. There are, however, few such task forces for other property-based cybercrimes and person-based offenses targeting adults. Such a force may be unrealistic at the local level due to diminished economic resources and few available trained staff.

If a task force model is untenable for the majority of local agencies, a better model would be to encourage the formation of large scale cybercrime specific units within major cities in a state that can also provide investigative resources and support to rural and outlying suburbs. In the event crimes are reported to sheriffs or local offices, this can provide a nearby resource that can aid in the investigation if it has a local nexus. Such a framework may promote a more favorable division of labor and encourage reporting generally.

In the event that such a model may be untenable due to the costs associated with large-scale task forces, there are alternatives that could be employed. For instance, the FBI operates Cyber Action Teams (CATs), which are highly trained small groups of agents, analysts, and forensic investigators who can respond to incidents around the world. These teams are designed to collect data and serve as rapid first responders to any incident, no matter where it occurs globally. While such a specialized team is helpful to respond to serious nation-state sponsored threats, it may be equally valuable to implement similar team structures using existing resources in local Bureau offices. Since there are offices across the U.S., designating trained agents who have the capability to respond to cybercrime cases could serve as on-site specialists for local police. They could be tasked to respond through either physical site visits or virtual consultations via Skype or other real-time video chat in order to aid investigators in proper search, seizure, and investigative techniques. This may provide local agencies with access to skilled and experienced investigators through cost-effective and efficient response mechanisms.

Another option may be to tap into state fusion centers, which are institutionalized task forces operated by state governments with support from federal agencies, namely the U.S. Department of Homeland Security. Fusion centers allow sharing of information across agencies as well as integrated decision making during natural or man-made disasters. Because the fusion centers focus on terrorism, their role in combating cybercrime would likely be limited to threats delivered via the Internet.

5) *Updated Laws*

In Chapter 4, we noted that local law enforcement felt that one of the most important ways to improve their response to cybercrime was through improved laws against cybercrime and increased prosecution of these offenses (Bossler & Holt, 2012). Virtually every state in the U.S. has legislation pertaining to various forms of cybercrime, whether under new or existing criminal statues (Brenner, 2011). The constantly evolving nature of technology makes it extremely difficult for legislators to develop laws either in advance of how a technology may be misused, or in such a way as to be broadly applicable to new offenses.

An excellent example of this challenge involves the problem of sexting, wherein people use the camera or video features contained on their smart phone or laptop to take and send photos or videos of themselves in provocative outfits or engage in sexually suggestive activities through text messaging (Mitchell, Finkelhor, Jones, & Wolak, 2012). Sexting has become popular as it is perceived as a way to attract or stimulate a prospective partner with a degree of security since it is directed toward only one recipient, rather than routed through an email client, which might make the content visible to others (Mitchell, Finkelhor, Jones, & Wolak, 2012).

Once the photo or video is sent it is no longer something that the sender can control. A recipient can easily circulate the content to others or repost the image on a social media site, like Facebook, to embarrass the sender (Mitchell et al., 2012). In addition, a number of websites have emerged where individuals can post sexual images and videos they received or acquired for others to see. These sites are often referred to as revenge porn and are facilitated by either former intimate partners who keep the images in the event a relationship sours, or by hacking someone's phone or email account in order to acquire pictures and embarrass the sender (Halloran, 2014).

The problem of sexting and the attendant misuse of images have led to substantive debates of the appropriate legal response to these activities. Since individuals voluntarily create and send the content to others, legislators have questioned whether they have any legal ownership or right to control where the content is used. Furthermore, some question whether it is appropriate to tie up local police resources for matters that may be more civil in nature. There has, however, been some agreement that law enforcement responses are needed in the event the person featured in the image is a minor. If the individual was coerced into taking photos by an adult, then it is sensible that child pornography charges be pursued (Jones et al., 2012). U.S. law enforcement agencies, mostly at the local level, have investigated 3,477 cases of sexting in 2008 and 2009 alone, though the proportion of cases involving adult recipients versus minor recipients are approximately the same (36 percent to 31 percent respectively; Wolak, Finkelhor, & Mitchell, 2012). Incidents involving adults were, however, much more likely to lead to an arrest (62 percent to 36 percent). Though this is a substantial number of cases, some researchers argue that criminalizing sexting may have more negative consequences for youth generally. Such a decision stigmatizes sexuality and promotes a knee-jerk response from policy makers rather than a thoughtful response that considers how legislation may further overtax criminal justice system actors (Jones et al., 2012). Thus, the need for new laws must be tempered with empirical research and attempts to understand a phenomenon before criminalizing and mandating investigation for what may be a minor problem.

There is also a need to determine the extent to which existing laws are successfully applied by local prosecutors and judges in the event that an investigation leads to an arrest. There is a substantial gap in our knowledge of this issue, as virtually no recent study has considered prosecutorial attitudes toward cybercrime and cybercrime law (e.g., Smith, Grabosky, & Urbas, 2002). Since there is generally little information on the extent to which cybercrime related complaints are investigated and cleared by arrest, it is unknown how well prosecutors understand the scope of cybercrime and how willing they are to pursue these cases. For instance, federal prosecutors are unlikely to continue investigations against actors living abroad as they may be unable to extradite or prosecute the individual in absentia (Peretti, 2009). As a result, some investigations are simply not pursued for fear that they will be viewed as a waste of resources. Similar issues may be present at the local level, as a prosecutor who believes cybercrime cases to be less pertinent to those involving homicides or drug crimes may be dropped. Scholarship is needed exploring this issue to better document the ways that criminal justice system actors view the problem of cybercrime and how their discretion affects the perception of these offenses among law enforcement.

6) *Cooperation with the High-Tech Industry*

As noted in Chapter 4, the line officers in our research generally indicated that public partnerships were not necessarily of value from their point of view. This is somewhat contradictory to the growing number of programs at the federal level that are designed to bring stakeholders from private industry together with law enforcement to review and discuss cybercrime threats. For instance, the FBI operates the InfraGard project which is a nationwide non-profit public-private partnership designed to facilitate information sharing between academics, industry, and law enforcement (InfraGard, 2013). There are chapters in each state in the U.S. InfraGard operates to aid in connecting private industry employees who may be the first to identify attacks against various resources together with federal law enforcement to understand who they should contact in the event of active threats. There are over 54,000 members of the group, including members of local law enforcement, all of whom must go through a vetting process in order to participate (InfraGard, 2013). In turn, members gain access to a secured web portal where intelligence on threats, vulnerabilities, and general information is shared.

Since local law enforcement agencies may not be contacted in the event of large scale hacking incidents or attacks against some parts of critical infrastructure, such a program may seem to have little value. There are other partnerships that could prove invaluable to facilitate cybercrime investigations and information sharing programs. For instance, linking local police with Internet Service Providers in the area, whether cable companies, cell phone providers, and even universities and public libraries, could be extremely important connections to ensure that these entities know one another and recognize how they may be able to work together to collect or retain evidence in the event that cybercrimes are identified. Similarly, connecting police with small business owners to discuss cybercrimes may be valuable to increase awareness of cybercrimes of any sort. For instance, small businesses may not experience wide scale data breaches, but their employees may misuse technological resources or be the first to notice unusual activities that may be signals of a cybercrime in progress. Linking these groups together may prove tremendously valuable to improve reporting of cybercrime and create conduits for information sharing on active and emergent threats.

7) *Special Research and Publications*

This work is an attempt to fill the gap in our knowledge of what state and local law enforcement need in order to better respond to cybercrime. Since this study comes more than a decade after the publication of the Stambaugh report (2001), and there has not been a dramatic increase in empirical research on the law enforcement response to cybercrime, it is necessary to know how we may rectify this issue. The substantial size of the population of state and local law enforcement agencies makes it difficult to simply survey officer attitudes in a way that captures a representative sample of patrol officers and management. As a result, much of the existing literature is based on convenience samples of police agencies in a single region rather than through nationally representative samples (e.g., Bossler & Holt, 2012; Hinduja, 2004; Holt & Bossler, 2012a, 2012b; Senjo, 2004).

There is a need for increased federal research grants specifically targeting cybercrime scholarship. Over the last decade, funding agencies such as the National Institute of Justice have increased research dollars to understand the scope of transnational organized crime and terrorism (e.g., Picarelli, 2012), though there have been no real targeted calls toward cybercrime. In fact, the only area of cybercrime scholarship that has been well-funded is research designed to address our knowledge of child sexual exploitation online through the Office of Juvenile Justice and Delinquency Prevention. Thus, federal research funds must be expanded if we are to improve the response capacity of law enforcement at the local level.

8) *Management Awareness and Support*

Our findings point to two interrelated issues with regard to management awareness and support for cybercrime investigation. The first relates to managerial support for cybercrime investigation among line officers and staff in local law enforcement agencies. The analyses presented in Chapter 3 illustrate that officer interest in cybercrime training was unaffected by managerial support for cybercrime investigation. This relationship may not hold constant in all areas of the country, or be generalizable to larger law enforcement agencies or cities with particularly high rates of violence or drug crimes. Future study is needed to understand the extent to which managerial support affects local officer attitudes toward cybercrime (e.g., Hinduja, 2004).

The second issue pertains specifically to policies regarding digital forensic investigators' occupational responses and traumatic experiences through analysis. The findings in Chapter 5 illustrate that digital forensic investigators share many common occupational experiences with employees of the larger criminal justice system. The results of the regression analyses for the predictors of stress and satisfaction provide multiple avenues for managers in crime laboratories or police agencies where digital forensic investigators operate. The implementation of clear policies that benefit investigators may be able to decrease levels of burnout, absenteeism, poor job performance, turnover, and physical and mental health problems (Holt & Blevins, 2011; Holt et al., 2012; Perez et al., 2009).

The findings of this study suggest there are several factors that laboratory directors and management should carefully target. First, the relationship between investigators' levels of job stress and satisfaction and their perceptions of supervisory and top management support indicate the need for well-defined policies and open lines of communication. Establishing clear lines of communication both up and down the chain of command can give investigators direct access to upper management and foster trust between all parties (Becker & Dale, 2003). The use of open staff meetings where management is present to hear concerns and needs of investigators may help to promote support for the scientific staff. In addition, the clear communication of justifications for supporting or denying equipment and training requests would be valuable to eliminate perceptions of detachment from management and clearly justify why certain issues are given priority over others.

Second, laboratory management may benefit from carefully revised staffing plans and written policies concerning scientific procedures in order to reduce redundancy and diminish the likelihood of role conflicts. Unlike some of the physical forensic sciences, there are multiple paths and tools that can be used to develop results from digital forensic evidence (e.g., Egohan & Casey, 2005). The lack of consistency can lead to unclear expectations and procedural standards which can increase individual levels of stress and decrease job satisfaction. Thus, identifying best practices and communicating these standards to all investigators, whether through training centers or across state agencies, can help to establish clear work roles and tasks that can be understood and achieved on a daily basis. Communicating requirements for the time needed to process evidence, appropriate avenues for contact with investigators and management, and expectations for analysis times are necessary to improve the occupational experiences of investigators and help solidify managerial support of scientists in their laboratories (National Academy of Sciences, 2009).

Third, laboratory directors and management should promote awareness of signs of emotional stress or secondary trauma among the investigators in their laboratories (Holt & Blevins, 2011; Israel et al., 1989; Jackson & Maslach, 1982; Perez et al., 2009). A number of respondents indicated that they experienced some physical symptoms of trauma as a result of their work, such as nightmares, irritability, feelings of alertness, or difficulty sleeping. The presence of these symptoms was more likely to be reported with higher levels of job stress and diminished when individuals reported higher levels of satisfaction. The same is true concerning the use of coping mechanisms to deal with work stress, though very few respondents reported engaging in serious negative strategies.

Because many secondary trauma symptoms directly reduce the productivity and general well-being of investigators, laboratory directors should encourage scientists to report when they experience these symptoms or any concerns about physical health. Management should also ensure that scientists are aware of the available mental health services, whether counselors or therapists, should they feel the need to speak with a professional to help express their concerns. Less than 10 percent of the scientists in this sample sometimes used professional assistance, in keeping with the rates identified in other studies of criminal justice systems employees (see Burns et al., 2008; Holt & Blevins,

2010; Perez et al., 2010). Ensuring that access to these resources are clearly communicated and encouraged when necessary, may have beneficial impacts on both stress and satisfaction and improve the overall working environment of the laboratory. Such strategies may dramatically improve the working conditions of digital forensic investigators and concurrently increase their efficacy over time.

9) *Investigative and Forensic Tools*

Though our study does not necessarily speak to the quality of forensic tools, we have clearly identified issues related to staffing analysts in the field in Chapter 5. Given the degree of stress associated with exposure to child exploitation images on a constant basis (Perez et al., 2009), it may be pivotal to develop automated tools to facilitate rapid analyses of content with minimal investigator interactions. Not only would such resources help to increase the number of child pornography cases that are handled at the local level, but also help reduce the potential for investigator burnout. To develop such resources, there is a need for criminologists, psychologists, and computer scientists to work together to develop tools that will most effectively address the needs of investigators.

To that end, there is also a need for researchers to regularly survey the investigator community to understand their perceptions of the current body of forensic analysis tools available, their limits, and the tools that may be needed to improve their ability to investigate cybercrime cases. There are few empirical assessments of the functionality of forensic analysis tools used by cybercrime investigators. As a result, it is difficult to know what tools comprise the best in the field and which are simply most commonly adopted. Working with the various entities that provide training to the law enforcement community, such as the NW3C, would be a vital way to identify these needs and gain access to investigators with varying degrees of experience.

10) *Structuring a Computer Crime Unit*

In Chapters 3 and 4, we examined what factors affect local officer's interest in cybercrime training and their attitudes toward responses to strategies to deal with cybercrime. Though training is an important issue, what may be even more pertinent is to expand the capacity of local agencies to investigate cybercrimes. Whether or not a police agency is large enough to maintain their own cybercrime unit, there is a need to find ways to better incorporate citizens into any responsive policing effort. The sheer size of the population who can serve as the eyes and ears, or community informants, for law enforcement would dramatically improve their ability to understand the general threat of cybercrimes and develop new leads for investigators.

Calling for innovative solutions to address cybercrime at the local level is much different, however, than actually implementing these programs. We possess generally little information on the structure of online community policing programs and how they would operate. Based on the basic tenets of community-oriented policing, we know that the need for citizen engagement will be critical. This may take two distinct forms in cyberspace: 1) citizens as engaged informants providing information about crime problems; and 2) community members working with police to identify problems and aid in solution creation.

Utilizing community members as sources of direct information on criminal activity has long been recognized as a valuable strategy to aid in cybercrime investigation (e.g., Brenner, 2008; Wall, 2001). Internet users comprise the largest group of eyes and ears on the Internet and can identity when cybercrime and other forms of online illicit behaviors occur (Wall, 2001). In addition, many online users have access to online communities that law enforcement personnel may not be aware of or have the time to fully examine to understand their operations. For instance, there are a range of sexual communities currently operating which could be used as a means to engage in illegal activities on or off-line. There are multiple forums currently used to discuss prostitution services available in cities across the U.S., driven in large part by the customers of sex workers (e.g., Cunningham & Kendall, 2013; Holt & Blevins, 2007; Milrod & Monto, 2012). These forums give direct information on the ways that individuals solicit sex and their use of technology to connect with sex workers on and off-line (Holt, Blevins, & Kuhns, 2014). These data sources may or may not be known or used by the law enforcement community to surreptitiously monitor the scope of prostitution, demonstrating the value in incorporating the community in order to understand various problems.

The same is true for the various technologies and applications that may be used by younger populations, such as Snapchat or dating apps like Grindr and Tinder. These applications are driven primarily by relationships, making it difficult to document online communications and behavior patterns unless officers are incorporated into these social networks. As a result, law enforcement agencies may only become aware of a threat in these unique application driven environments if they are reported. Community members can serve as pivotal points of contact into various online communities and can act as informants and as early warning systems to potential problems.

In this respect, community members may be linked into cybercrime investigations through various ways. One of the most immediate and simple resources may be the creation of online tip services designed to allow citizens to report suspicious online behavior directly to law enforcement. This may be easily linked through social media to local police resources, whether through Twitter or Facebook, which could be managed by a resource or communications officer within the agency. These comments would undoubtedly have to be prioritized and investigated further, but could provide direct information to local agencies that may stimulate leads and cases. In fact, the National Center for Missing and Exploited Children operates a CyberTipline which provides an electronic resource for individuals to report suspected incidents of child abuse, child pornography, and sexual exploitation. This could serve as a model for local agencies, as the Tipline has generated over 2.2 million reports of prospective abuse since its implementation in 1998 (National Center for Missing and Exploited Children, 2014).

Promotion and management of a tip line is just one facet of what would undoubtedly be a complex approach to virtual community-oriented policing. In addition, officers would have to directly connect with the community through virtual and real meetings to promote awareness of the problem of cybercrime and unite the community around issues of interest to them. For instance, mobilizing community watch groups and civic organizations in the real world to meet to discuss cybercrime and cybersecurity issues would be a valuable first step in demonstrating that local police not only care about this problem but also want to proactively deal with threats. In addition, school resource officers could be used as a means to communicate cybercrime concerns to youth, along with safe surfing habits and the recognition that if someone does something wrong, they can contact police for help.

Once local communities recognize that local law enforcement can be mobilized to deal with certain forms of cybercrime, this may increase the efficacy and use of the virtual tip lines and potentially increase reports through traditional 911 services. In addition, law enforcement may be able to further mobilize local community groups to also patrol online spaces for wrongdoing and report observed behavior when needed. This would enhance the value of tip line complaints as they may have greater information to legitimize or justify a complaint made to police. Finally, establishing a social media presence for cybercrime cases and threat information that may be of value to the local community would be imperative to help continually update the community on what risks they may face from malware, hacking, or fraud. In turn, this may increase the general cybersecurity awareness of the community and minimize the risk of victimization from some forms of cybercrime.

The type of program outlined above is just one example of how a virtual community-oriented policing program may work. It is unclear how many such programs are currently active in the United States, or to what extent programs have been implemented and subsequently abandoned due to a lack of interest. There are a number of examples of cybercrime tip lines and social media-based platforms for information sharing and law enforcement interaction in an international context. For instance, the Finnish NetPolice operate as a community policing unit for online spaces by operating a social media feed via Facebook and Twitter that is manned by an officer 24 hours a day (Forss, 2014). The officer interacts with the community for traditional communications and can also accept criminal complaints and even issue warnings to individual users on the basis of their posting behaviors while online (Forss, 2014). This is, however, a relatively novel approach that may not be possible to implement in a nation as large and economically diverse as the United States. Though a local sheriff's office may be able to maintain a social media profile, it is unlikely that it can be staffed 24 hours a day or used to proactively police posts due to not only the cost but also concerns over limiting individual freedoms of speech online.

The community policing paradigm goes beyond police-community relations. A central tenet of community policing is problem solving or problem-oriented policing, which asks officers to address community problems by finding solutions to crime and disorder via the root causes. For example, officers patrolling a neighborhood where teenage cruising is causing a rise in complaints would seek out the causes of the cruising: Who is doing it? Why in this area? Why now? A law-enforcement model would simply arrest the offenders, while a problem-solving model would look for causes and address those problems first, such as redirecting the traffic flow by closing off certain streets. With regard to cybercrime, officers using a problem-oriented policing model would look for multiple responses to the problem, but they must be attentive to cybercrimes as part of their patrol activities. The Center for Problem-Oriented Policing, for instance, provides an example of such strategies through their guide for child pornography on the Internet (Wortley & Smallbone, 2006).

As a result, there is a need for substantive research in order to not only assess how the community may feel about the implementation of virtual community policing initiatives, but also to evaluate any existing programs to understand their process and efficacy. The relatively novel nature of community policing online means that they may have developed in the absence of empirically derived evidence or proven strategies to deal with cybercrime. These conditions make it vital that researchers understand the motivations and principles that led to one program over another. Since programs may have been designed by a small number of officers, researchers may benefit from employing mixed methods of interviews with officers and surveys of the public to more completely assess the scope and success of any intervention.

Limitations and Conclusions

Despite the valuable implications of this study for the practitioner community, there are several key limitations that must be recognized. Though our research is driven by empirical investigation which is extremely rare in the current literature on policing cybercrimes, the data used throughout this work are based on limited samples. The data generated from Charlotte and Savannah line officers may not be generalizable to all regions of the country. While both of these cities have served as research sites for line officer decision making (Alpert et al., 2005), stress (Lord, 1996), and police impact on citizens' fear of crime (Rutherford et al., 2009), they can only serve as prospective barometers for larger trends in policing. Further research is needed from police agencies of all sizes that serve small, medium, and large communities. Such research would validate perceptual differences on the basis of existing resources and citizen technology use generally.

In much the same way, the samples of forensic investigators from law enforcement agencies must be carefully considered. We utilized convenience samples of investigators who have gone through a training program sequence offered by the National White Collar Crime Center. There are several other national resources that provide training to digital forensic investigators and their access to trainee samples may be extremely valuable to assess the generalizability of these findings. Furthermore, we focused on the working experiences of investigators, but substantive research is needed to refine our understanding of the technical needs and case experiences that affect their daily operation. At the same time, the limitations in all of the data sources used in this work are consistent with those noted across the existing literature on policing attitudes toward cybercrime generally. Low response rates are evident in various national samples of local law enforcement agencies (Burns et al., 2004; Marcum et al., 2010), while many studies are extremely limited to samples from single states within the United States (Hinduja, 2004; Senjo, 2004).

Taken as a whole, this work demonstrates the vital role that local police may serve in the investigation and enforcement of cybercrimes. While there is mixed support for the investigation of these offenses, officers recognize that these crimes occur and are equal in severity relative to some street crimes. Officers must be appropriately engaged in their role as first responders, though they may not necessarily value working with the general public to help deal with the problem of cybercrime in their community. Thus, care must be taken to select officers for specialized investigative roles based on their attitudes and perceptions, not simply because of youth or technological savvy.

It is also necessary to recognize that digital forensic investigators may become increasingly prominent players in cybercrime cases over the next decade. The difficult tasks they must deal with in the course of their jobs demands careful management and staffing to minimize burnout and increase employee retention over time. This work is, however, a first step toward enhancing our understanding of cybercrime at the local level. A great deal of research is still needed to not only validate, but also expand and improve upon, our findings to better understand offending in the 21st century.

References

Abdollahi, M. K. (2002). Understanding police stress research. *Journal of Forensic Practice, 2,* 1–24.

Adams, R.E., Rohe, W.M., & Arcury, T.A. (2002). Implementing community-oriented policing: Organizing change and street officer attitudes. *Crime and Delinquency, 48,* 399–430.

Alkus, S., & Padesky, C. (1983). Special problems of police officers: Stress related issues and interventions. *Counseling Psychologist, 11,* 55–64.

Alpert, G.P., Macdonald, J.M., & Dunham, R.G. (2005). Police suspicion and discretionary decision making during citizen stops. *Criminology, 43,* 407–434.

Andress, J., & Winterfeld, S. (2011). *Cyber Warfare: Techniques, Tactics, and Tools for Security Practitioners.* Waltham MA: Syngress.

Anshel, M., Robertson, M., & Caputi, P. (1997). Sources of acute stress and their appraisals and reappraisals among Australian police as a function of previous experience. *Journal of Occupational and Organizational Psychology, 70,* 337–356.

Bachmann, M. (2010). The Risk Propensity and Rationality of Computer Hackers. *The International Journal of Cyber Criminology, 4,* 643–656.

Baum, K. (2004). *First estimates from the National Crime Victimization Survey: Identity Theft, 2004.* Washington D.C.: U.S. Department of Justice, Office of Justice Statistics. Retrieved from April 15, 2007, from http://www.ojp.usdoj.gov/bjs/pub/pdf/it04.pdf

Bayley, D. H. (1998). *What works in policing.* New York: Oxford University Press.

Bayley, D., & Shearing, C. (1996). The future of policing. *Law and Society Review, 30,* 585–606.

Becker, W. S., & Dale, W. M. (2003). Strategic human resource management in the forensic science laboratory. *Forensic Science Communications, 5.*

Belknap, J., & Shelly, J. K. (1992). The new lone ranger: Police women on patrol. *American Journal of Policing, 12,* 47–73.

Bickart, B., & Schmittlein, D. (1999). The distribution of survey contact and participation in the United States: Constructing a survey-based estimate. *Journal of Marketing Research, 36,* 286–294.

Blevins, K. R., Cullen, F. T., Frank, J., Sundt, J. L., & Holmes, S. T. (2007). Stress and satisfaction among juvenile correctional workers: A test of competing models. *Journal of Offender Rehabilitation, 44,* 55–79.

Bocij, P. (2004). *Cyberstalking: Harassment in the Internet age and how to protect your family.* Westport, CT: Praeger.

Bossler, A. M., & Holt, T. J. (2009). On-line activities, guardianship, and malware infection: An examination of routine activities theory. *International Journal of Cyber Criminology, 3,* 400–420.

Bossler, A. M., & Holt, T. J. (2012). Patrol officers' perceived role in responding to cybercrime. *Policing: An International Journal of Police Strategies & Management, 35,* 165–181.

Bossler, A. M., & Holt, T. J. (2013). Assessing officer perceptions and support for online community policing. *Security Journal, 26,* 349–366.

Bossler, A. M., & Holt, T. J. (2014). Further examining officer perceptions and support for online community policing. In C. Marcum & G. Higgins (Eds.) *Social networking as a criminal enterprise* (pp. 167–196). London: Taylor & Francis.

Braga, A. A. (2008). Pulling Levers Focused Deterrence Strategies and the Prevention of Gun Homicide. *Journal of Criminal Justice, 36,* 332–343.

Brenner, S. W. (2008). *Cyberthreats: The Emerging Fault Lines of the Nation State.* New York: Oxford University Press.

Brenner, S. W. (2011). Defining Cybercrime: A Review of Federal and State Law. In R. D. Clifford (Ed.), *Cybercrime: The investigation, prosecution, and defense of a computer-related crime, 3rd Edition* (pp. 15–104). Durham, NC: Carolina Academic Press.

Britz, M. T. (2010). Terrorism and technology: Operationalizing cyberterrorism and identifying concepts. In T. J. Holt (Ed.), *Crime On-Line: Correlates, Causes, and Context* (pp. 193–220). Durham, NC: Carolina Academic Press, 2010.

Brodsky, J., & Radvanovsky, R. (2011). Control Systems Security. In T. J. Holt & B. Schell (Eds.), *Corporate Hacking and Technology-Driven Crime: Social Dynamics and Implications.* (pp. 187–204) Hershey, PA: IGI-Global.

Bureau of Labor Statistics. (2009). *Current population survey, 2008.* Washington, DC: Bureau of Labor Statistics. Retrieved July 15, 2010, from http://www.bls.gov/cps/demographics.htm.

Burke, R. J., & Mikkelsen, A. (2005). Gender issues in policing: Do they matter? *Women in Management Review, 20*, 133–143.

Burns, C. M., Morley, J., Bradshaw, R., & Domene, J. (2008). The emotion impact on and coping strategies employed by police teams investigating Internet child exploitation. *Traumatology, 14*, 20–31.

Burns, R. G., Whitworth, K.H., & Thompson, C.Y. (2004). Assessing law enforcement preparedness to address Internet fraud. *Journal of Criminal Justice, 32*, 477–493.

Business Software Alliance. (2012). *Shadow Market: 2011 BSA Global Software Piracy Study*. Accessed April 10, 2013, from http://globalstudy.bsa.org/2011/downloads/study_pdf/2011_BSA_Piracy_Study-Standard.pdf.

Castle, T. L. (2008). Satisfied in the jail? Exploring the predictors of job satisfaction among jail officers. *Criminal Justice Review, 33*, 48–63.

Catalano, S. (2012). *Stalking Victims in the United States-Revised*. Washington, D.C.: U.S. Department of Justice. Retrieved July 12, 2013 from http://www.bjs.gov/content/pub/pdf/svus_rev.pdf.

Central Intelligence Agency. (2011). *The World Factbook 2011*. Washington, DC: Central Intelligence Agency. Retrieved October 20, 2013, from https://www.cia.gov/library/publications/the-world-factbook/index.html.

Cere, R. (2003). Digital counter-cultures and the nature of electronic social and political movements. In Y. Jewkes (Ed.), *Dot.cons: Crime, deviance and identity on the Internet.* (pp. 147–163). Portland, OR: Willan Publishing.

Coman, G., & Evans, B. (1991). Stressors facing Australian police in the 1990s. *Police Studies, 14*, 153–165.

Computer Security Institute. (2009). Computer Crime and Security Survey. Retrieved June 3, 2010 from http://www.cybercrime.gov/FBI2009.pdf.

Cordner, G. W. (1999). Elements of community policing. In L. K. Gaines & G. W. Cordner (Eds.), *Policing Perspectives: An Anthology* (pp. 137–149). Los Angeles: Roxbury.

Cullen, F. T., Lemming, T., Link, B. G., & Wozniak, J. F. (1985). The impact of social supports on police stress. *Criminology, 23*, 503–522.

Cullen, F. T., Lutze, F., Link, B. G., & Wolfe, N. T. (1989). The correctional orientation of prison guards: Do officers support rehabilitation? *Federal Probation, 53*, 33–42.

Cunningham, S., & Kendall, T. (2013). Sex for sale: Online commerce in the world's oldest profession. In T. J. Holt (Ed.), *Crime On-line: Correlates, causes, and context, 2nd Edition* (pp. 40–75). Durham, NC: Carolina Academic Press.

Dantzer, M. L. (1987). Police related stress: A critique for future research. *Journal of Police and Criminal Psychology, 9*, 43–48.

Davidson, M. J., & Veno, A. (1980). Stress and the policeman. In C. L. Cooper & J. Marshall (Eds.), *White collar and professional stress* (pp. 131–166). New York: John Wiley & Sons.

Denning, D. E. (2011). Cyber-conflict as an Emergent Social Problem. In T. J. Holt & B. Schell (Eds.), *Corporate Hacking and Technology-Driven Crime: Social Dynamics and Implications.* (pp. 170–186). Hershey, PA: IGI-Global.

Department of Energy. (2013). *National Security and Safety.* Retrieved January 20, 2014 from http://energy.gov/public-services/national-security-safety.

Dey, E. L. (1997). Working with low survey response rates: The efficacy of weighting adjustments. *Research in Higher Education, 38*, 97–114.

Dignam, J. T., Barrera, M., & West, S.G. (1986). Occupational stress, social support, and burnout among correctional officers. *American Journal of Community Psychology, 14*, 177–193.

Dowler, K. (2005). Job satisfaction, burnout, and perception of unfair treatment: The relationship between race and police work. *Police Quarterly, 8*, 476–489.

Durkin, K. F. (1997). Misuse of the Internet by pedophiles: Implications for law enforcement and probation practice. *Federal Probation, 14*, 14–18.

Durkin, K. F., & Bryant, C. D. (1999). Propagandizing pederasty: A thematic analysis of the online exculpatory accounts of unrepentant pedophiles. *Deviant Behavior, 20*, 103–127.

Edleman, B. (2009). Red Light States: Who Buys Online Adult Entertainment? *Journal of Economic Perspectives, 23*, 209–220.

Eisenberg, T. (1975). Labor-management relations and psychological stress: View from the bottom. *The Police Chief, 42*, 54–58.

Ellison, K. W., & Genz, J. (1983). *Stress and the police officer.* Springfield, IL: Charles C Thomas.

Esbensen, F. A., Osgood, D. W., Peterson, D., Taylor, T. J., & Carson, D. C. (2013). Short and Long Term Outcome Results from a Multi-site Evaluation of the G.R.E.A.T. Program. *Criminology and Public Policy.*

Facebook. (2013). Facebook reports first quarter 2013 results. Retrieved October 12, 2014 from http://investor.fb.com/releasedetail.cfm?ReleaseID=761090.

Facebook. (2013). *Safety.* Retrieved June 1, 2014 from http://www.facebook.com/safety/tools/.

Federal Bureau of Investigation. (2000). *National Incident-Based Reporting System: Volume 1: Data Collection Guidelines.* Retrieved June 15, 2014 from http://www2.fbi.gov/ucr/nibrs/manuals/v1all.pdf.

Federal Bureau of Investigation. (2004). *Uniform Crime Reporting Handbook.* US Department of Justice: Washington D.C. Retrieved April 15, 2014 from http://www.fbi.gov/about-us/cjis/ucr/additional-ucr-publications/ucr_handbook.pdf.

Federal Law Enforcement Training Center. (2012). *Internet Investigations Training Program (IITP).* Retrieved August 1, 2013 from http://www.fletc.gov/training/programs/investigative-operations-division/economic-financial/internet-investigations-training-program-iitp/?searchterm=cybercrime.

Ferraro, M., & Casey, E. (2005). *Investigating child exploitation and pornography: The internet, the law, and forensic science.* New York, NY: Elsevier Academic Press.

Finkelhor, D. (2008). *Childhood Victimization: Violence, Crime, and Abuse in the Lives of Young People.* New York: Oxford University Press.

Finkelhor, D., & Ornod, R. (2004). Child pornography: Patterns from NIBRS. *OJJDP Juvenile Justice Bulletin.* Retrieved June 20, 2014 from https://www.ncjrs.gov/pdffiles1/ojjdp/204911.pdf?q=pornography.

Finkelhor, D., Mitchell, K. J., & Wolak, J. (2000). *Online victimization: A report on the nation's youth.* Washington DC: National Center for Missing and Exploited Children.

Finn, J. (2004). A Survey of Online Harassment at a University Campus. *Journal of Interpersonal Violence, 19,* 468–483.

Foltz, B. C. (2004). Cyberterrorism, computer crime, and reality. *Information Management & Computer Security 12,* 154–166.

Forss, M. (2010). *Virtual community policing.* Retrieved June 1, 2012 from http://www.slideshare.net/fobba/virtual-community-policing-3938294.

Foster, R. E. (2005). *Police technology.* Upper Saddle River, NJ: Pearson Prentice Hall.

Furnell, S. (2002). *Cybercrime: Vandalizing the Information Society.* London: Addison-Wesley.

Ganster, D. C., Fusilier, M., & Mayes, B.T. (1986). Role of social support in the experience of stress at work. *Journal of Applied Psychology, 71,* 102–110.

Golembiewski, R.T., & Kim, B. (1990). Burnout in police work: Stressors, strain, and the phase model. *Police Studies, 13,* 74–80.

Goodman, M.D. (1997). Why the police don't care about computer crime. *Harvard Journal of Law and Technology, 10,* 465–494.

Grabosky, P. (2007). *Electronic Crime,* Pearson Prentice Hall, Upper Saddle River, NJ.

Graf, F.A. (1986). The relationship between social support and occupational stress among police officers. *Journal of Police Science and Administration, 14,* 178–186.

Grossi, E., Keil, T., & G. Vito. (1996). Surviving the joint: Mitigating factors of correctional officer stress. *Journal of Crime and Justice, 19,* 103–120.

Gruen, M. (2005). Innovative Recruitment and Indoctrination Tactics by Extremists: Video Games, Hip Hop, and the World Wide Web. In J. J. Forest (Ed.) *The Making of a Terrorist,* (pp. 25–40). Westport, CT: Praeger.

Gunter, W. D. (2009). Internet scallywags: A comparative analysis of multiple forms and measurements of digital piracy. *Western Criminology Review, 10,* 15–28.

Haarr, R., & Morash, M. (1999). Gender, race, and strategies of coping with occupational stress in policing. *Justice Quarterly, 16,* 303–336.

Hagy, D. W. (2007). *Digital evidence in the courtroom: A guide for law enforcement and prosecutors.* U.S. Department of Justice: Washington D.C.

Halloran, L. (2014). Race to stop "Revenge Porn" raises free speech worries. March 6, 2014. National Public Radio. Retrieved June 3, 2014 from www.npr.org/blogs/itsallpolitics/2014/03/06/286388840/race-to-stop-revenge-porn-raises-free-speech-worries.

Harocopos, A., & Hough, M. (2005). Drug dealing in open-air markets. Department of Justice, Office of Community Oriented Policing, Washington D.C.

He, N., Zhao, J., & Archbold, C. A. (2002). Gender and police stress: The convergent and divergent impact of work environment, work-family conflict, and stress coping mechanisms of female and male police officers. *Policing: An International Journal of Police Strategies & Management, 25,* 687–708.

Hickman, M. J., & Reaves, B. A. (2006). *Local Police Departments, 2003.* Bureau of Justice Statistics. Washington, D.C.; US Department of Justice. Retrieved April 1, 2014 from http://www.bjs.gov/content/pub/pdf/lpd03.pdf.

Higgins, G. E. (2005). Can low self-control help with the understanding of the software piracy problem? *Deviant Behavior, 26,* 1–24.

Higgins, K. J. (2014). Target, Neiman Marcus Data Breaches Tip of the Iceberg. *Dark Reading,* January 13, 2014. Retrieved February 17, 2014 from (http://

www.darkreading.com/attacks-breaches/target-neiman-marcus-data-breaches-tip-o/240165363).

Hinduja, S. (2004). Perceptions of local and state law enforcement concerning the role of computer crime investigative teams. *Policing: An International Journal of Police Strategies and Management, 3,* 341–357.

Hinduja, S. (2007). Computer crime investigations in the United States: Leveraging knowledge from the past to address the future. *International Journal of Cyber Criminology, 1,* 1–26.

Hinduja, S., & Patchin, J. W. (2009). *Bullying beyond the schoolyard: Preventing and responding to cyberbullying.* New York: Corwin Press.

Hinduja, S., & Patchin, J. W. (2012). *Summary of Cyberbullying Research From 2004–2012.* Retrieved December 2, 2013 from Available at: http://cyberbullying.us/research.

Hoffman, B. (2006). *Inside Terrorism.* New York: Columbia University Press.

Holt, T. J. (2003). Examining a transnational problem: An analysis of computer crime victimization in eight countries from 1999 to 2001. *International Journal of Comparative and Applied Criminal Justice, 27,* 199–220.

Holt, T. J. (2007). Subcultural evolution? Examining the influence of on- and off-line experiences on deviant subcultures. *Deviant Behavior, 28,* 171–198.

Holt, T. J. (2012). Exploring the intersections of technology, crime and terror. *Terrorism and Political Violence, 24,* 337–354.

Holt, Thomas J. (2013). Examining the Forces Shaping Cybercrime Markets Online. *Social Science Computer Review, 31,* 165–177.

Holt, T. J., & Blevins, K. R. (2007). Examining sex work from the client's perspective: Assessing johns using online data. *Deviant Behavior, 28,* 333–354.

Holt, T. J., & Blevins, K. R. (2012). Examining job stress and satisfaction among digital forensic examiners. *Journal of Contemporary Criminal Justice, 27,* 230–250.

Holt, T. J., Blevins, K. R., & Burkert, N. (2010). Considering the pedophile subculture on-line. *Sexual Abuse: Journal of Research and Treatment, 22,* 3–24.

Holt, T. J., & Bossler, A. M. (2012a). Police perceptions of computer crimes in two southeastern cities: An examination from the viewpoint of patrol officers. *American Journal of Criminal Justice, 37,* 396–412.

Holt, T. J., & Bossler, A. M. (2012b). Predictors of patrol officer interest in cybercrime training and investigation in selected United States Police Departments. *Cyberpsychology, Behavior, and Social Networking, 15,* 464–472.

Holt, T. J., & Bossler, A. M. (2014). An assessment of the current state of cybercrime scholarship. *Deviant Behavior, 35*, 20–40.

Holt, T. J., Bossler, A. M., & Fitzgerald, S. (2010). Examining state and local law enforcement perceptions of computer crime. In T. J. Holt, (Ed.) *Crime On-line: Correlates, causes, and context* (pp. 221–246). Durham, NC: Carolina Academic Press.

Holt, T. J., & Graves, D. C. (2007). A Qualitative Analysis of Advanced Fee Fraud Schemes. *The International Journal of Cyber-Criminology, 1*, 137–154.

House, J. S. (1981). *Work Stress and Social Support*. Reading, MA: Addison-Wesley.

Hunt, R. G., & McCadden, K. S. (1985). A survey of work attitudes of police officers: Commitment and satisfaction. *Police Studies, 8*, 17–25.

InfraGard. (2013). *InfraGard in the News*. Retrieved July 20, 2014 from https://www.infragard.org/.

International Association of Chiefs of Police. (2009). 2008 IACP Community Policing Awards: Presented at the 115th Annual IACP Conference. *The Police Chief, 77*. Retrieved April 1, 2011 from http://policechiefmagazine.org/magazine/index.cfm?fuseaction=display_arch&article_id=1749&issue_id=32009.

Internet Crime Complaint Center. (2010). *IC3 2009 Internet Crime Report*. Retrieved March 24, 2010 from http://www.ic3.gov/media/annualreport/2009_IC3Report.pdf.

Internet Crime Complaint Center. (2014), *IC3 2014 Internet Crime Report*. Retrieved October 20, 2014 from http://www.ic3.gov/media/annualreport/20134_IC3Report.pdf.

Internet Crimes Against Children Task Force. (2014). *Internet Crimes Against Children Task Force Program*. Retrieved May 20, 2014 from https://www.icactaskforce.org/Pages/ICACTFP.aspx.

Jenkins, P. (2001). *Beyond tolerance: Child pornography on the Internet*. New York: New York University Press.

Johnson, S., Cooper, C., Cartwright, S., Donald, I., Taylor, P., & Millet, C. (2005). The experience of work-related stress across occupations. *Journal of Managerial Psychology, 20*, 178–187.

Jones, B. R. (2007). Comment: Virtual neighborhood watch: Open source software and community policing against cybercrime. *Journal of Criminal Law and Criminology, 97*, 601–630.

Jones, L. M., Mitchell, K. J., & Finkelhor, D. (2012). Trends in Youth Internet Victimization: Findings From Three Youth Internet Safety Surveys 2000–2010. *Journal of Adolescent Health, 50*, 179–186.

Jones, L. M., Mitchell, K., Wolak, J., & Finkelhor, D. (2013). Online harassment in context: Trends from three youth Internet safety surveys (2000, 2005, 2010). *Psychology of Violence, 3,* 53–69.

Jordan, T., & Taylor, P. (1998). A Sociology of Hackers. *The Sociological Review, 46,* 757–80.

King, A., & Thomas, J. (2009). You can't cheat an honest man: Making ($$$s and) sense of the Nigerian e-mail scams. In F. Schmalleger & M. Pittaro (Eds.) *Crime of the Internet* (pp. 206–224). Saddle River, NJ: Prentice Hall.

Kirkcaldy, B., Brown, J., & Cooper C. (1998). The demographics of occupational stress among police superintendents. *Journal of Managerial Psychology, 13,* 90–98.

Kohan, A, & Mazmanian, D. (2003). Police work, burnout, and pro-organizational behavior: A consideration of daily work experiences. *Criminal Justice and Behavior, 30,* 559–583.

Krause, M. (2009). Identifying and managing stress in child pornography and child exploitation investigators. *Journal of Police and Criminal Psychology, 24,* 22–29.

Krimmel, J. T., & Gormley, P. E. (2003). Tokenism and job satisfaction for police women. *American Journal of Criminal Justice, 28,* 73–88.

Kroes, W. H. (1985). *Society's victim—the policeman—an analysis of job stress in policing* (2nd ed.). New York: Charles C. Thomas.

Lane, F. S. (2000). *Obscene Profits: The Entrepreneurs of Pornography in the Cyber Age.* New York: Routledge.

Langton, L. (2011). *Identity theft reported by households 2005–2010.* Washington D.C.: US Department of Justice, Bureau of Justice Statistics.

LEMAS. (2010). *Law Enforcement Management and Administrative Statistics 2010.* Washington D.C.: United States Department of Justice, Office of Justice Statistics.

Lenhart, A., & Madden, M. (2007). *Teens, Privacy, and Online Social Networks.* Pew Internet and American Life Project. Retrieved November 11, 2011 from http://www.pewinternet.org/Reports/2007/Teens-Privacy-and-Online-Social-Networks.aspx.

Levy, S. (1984). *Hackers: Heroes of the Computer Revolution.* New York: Dell.

Lim, V. K., & Teo, T. S. (1998). Effects of individual characteristics on police officers' work-related attitudes. *Journal of Managerial Psychology, 13*, 334–342.

Liou, K. T. (1995). Role stress and job stress among detention care workers. *Criminal Justice and Behavior, 22*, 425–436.

Lord, V. B. (1996), An impact of community policing: Reported stressors, social support, and strain among police officers in a changing police department. *Journal of Criminal Justice, 24*, 503–522.

Lurigio, A. J., & Skogan, W. G. (1994). Winning the hearts and minds of police officers: an assessment of staff perceptions of community policing in Chicago. *Crime and Delinquency, 40*, 315–330.

Maguire, E. R. (2002). *Organizational Structure in Large Police Organizations: Context, Complexity, and Control.* SUNY Press, Albany, NY.

Maguire, E. R., & Shin, Y. (2003). Structural change in large police agencies during the 1990s. *Policing: An International Journal of Police Strategies and Management, 26*, 251–275.

Mandiant. (2013). *APT1: Exposing one of china's cyber espionage units.* Mandiant. Retrieved June 1, 2013 from http://intelreport.mandiant.com/.

Marcum, C., & Higgins, G. E. (2011). Combating child exploitation online: Predictors of successful ICAC task forces. *Policing: A Journal of Policy and Practice, 5*, 310–316.

Marcum, C., Higgins, G. E., Freiburger, T. L., & Ricketts, M. L. (2010). Policing possession of child pornography online: Investigating the training and resources dedicated to the investigation of cyber crime. *International Journal of Police Science & Management, 12*, 516–525.

Marshall, E. K. (2006). Cumulative career traumatic stress: A pilot study of traumatic stress in law enforcement. *Journal of Police and Criminal Psychology, 21*, 62–71.

Martelli, T. A., Waters, L. K., & Martelli, J. (1989). The police stress survey: Reliability and relation to job satisfaction and organizational commitment. *Psychological Reports, 64*, 267–273.

Martin, G. (2006). *Understanding terrorism: Challenges, perspectives, and issues, 2nd Edition.* Thousand Oaks, CA: Sage.

Mastrofski, S. D., Worden, R. E., & Snipes, J. B. (1995). Law enforcement in a time of community policing. *Criminology, 33*, 539–563.

McGarrell, E.F., Chermak, S., Wilson, J. M., & Corsaro, N. (2006). Reducing Homicide Through a "Lever-Pulling" Strategy. *Justice Quarterly, 23*, 214–231.

McGrath, M. G. & Casey, E. (2002). Forensic psychiatry and the internet: practical perspectives on sexual predators and obsessional harassers in cyberspace. *Journal of the American Academy of Psychiatry Law, 1,* 81–94.

McQuade, S. (2006). Technology-enabled crime, policing and security. *Journal of Technology Studies, 32,* 32–42.

Miller, S. (1999). *Gender and community policing: Walking the talk.* Boston: Northeastern University Press.

Milrod, C., & Weitzer, R. (2012). The Intimacy Prism: Emotion management among the clients of escorts. *Men and Masculinities, 15,* 447–467.

Mitchell, K. J., Finkelhor, D., Jones, L. M., and Wolak, J. (2012). Prevalence and characteristics of youth sexting: A national study. *Pediatrics, 129,* 13–20.

Mitchell, K. J., & Jones, L. M. (2013). *Internet-facilitated commercial sexual exploitation of children.* Crimes Against Children Research Center.

Mizota, K. (2013). Unbiased Testing Confirms: EnCase Forensic is Fastest. *Digital Forensics Today,* May 14, 2013. Retrieved July 2, 2014 from http://encase-forensic-blog.guidancesoftware.com/2013/05/unbiased-testing-confirms-encase_14.html.

Morash, M., Haarr, R., & Kwak, D. (2006). Multilevel influences on police stress. *Journal of Contemporary Criminal Justice, 22,* 26–43.

National Academy of Sciences. (2009). *Strengthening forensic science in the United States: A path forward.* Washington, D.C.: U.S. Department of Justice.

National Center for Missing and Exploited Children. (2014). *FAQs.* Retrieved June 1, 2014, from http://www.missingkids.com/Missing/FAQ.

National Institute of Justice. (2008). *Electronic Crime Scene Investigations: A Guide for First Responders,* 2nd ed., NCJ 219941, National Institute of Justice; Washington, D.C.

National Security Agency. (2013). *Mission Statement.* Retrieved November 1, 2013 from http://www.nsa.gov/about/mission/index.shtml.

National White Collar Crime Center. (2014). *State-of-the-Art Training.* Retrieved October 1, 2014 from http://www.nw3c.org/training.

Nazario, J. (2003). *Defense and detection strategies against Internet worms.* Artech House.

Newman, G., & Clarke, R. (2003). *Superhighway robbery: Preventing e-commerce crime.* Cullompton, NJ: Willan Press.

Nhan, J. (2013). The evolution of online piracy: Challenge and response. In T. J. Holt (Ed.). *Crime On-line: Causes, correlates, and context,* (pp. 61–80), Durham, NC: Carolina Academic Press.

Nobles, M. R., Reyns, B. W., Fox, K. A., & Fisher, B. S. (2012). Protection against pursuit: A conceptual and empirical comparison of cyberstalking and Stalking victimization among a national sample. *Justice Quarterly, 6,* 1–29.

Noblet, A., Rodwell, J., & Allisey, A. (2009). Job stress in the law enforcement sector: Comparing the linear, non-linear and interaction effects of working conditions. *Stress and Health: Journal of the International Society for the Investigation of Stress, 25,* 111–120.

Novak, K. J., Alarid, L. F., & Lucas, W. L. (2003). Exploring officers' acceptance of community policing: Implications for policy implementation. *Journal of Criminal Justice, 31,* 57–71.

Paoline, E. A., Myers, S. M., & Worden, R. E. (2000). Police culture, individualism, and community policing: Evidence from two police departments. *Justice Quarterly, 17,* 575–606.

Patterson, G. T. (2003). Examining the effects of coping on work and life stress among police officers. *Journal of Criminal Justice, 31,* 315–226.

Pelfrey, W. V. (2004). The inchoate nature of community policing: Differences between community policing and traditional police officers. *Justice Quarterly, 21,* 579–601.

Peretti, K. K. (2009). Data breaches: What the underground world of "carding" reveals. *Santa Clara Computer and High Technology Law Journal, 25,* 375–413.

Perez, L. M., Jones, J., Engler, D. R., & Sachau, D. (2010). Secondary traumatic stress and burnout among law enforcement investigators exposed to disturbing media images. *Journal of Police and Criminal Psychology, 25,* 113–124.

Petrone, S., & Reiser, M. (1985). A home visit program for stressed police officers. *The Police Chief, 52,* 36–37.

Picarelli, J. (2012). Osama bin Corleone? Vito the Jackal? Framing Threat Convergence Through an Examination of Transnational Organized Crime and International Terrorism. *Terrorism and Political Violence, 24,* 180–198.

Piquero, N. L. (2005). Understanding police stress and coping resources across gender: A look toward general strain theory. In H. Copes (Ed.), *Policing and Stress* (pp. 126–139). Upper Saddle River, NJ: Pearson Education.

Pollitt, M. M. (1998). Cyberterrorism—fact or fancy? *Computer Fraud & Security, 2,* 8–10.

Prensky, M. (2001). Digital Natives, Digital Immigrants. On the Horizon, October 2001, 9 (5). Lincoln: NCB University Press. Retrieved June 1, 2013, from http://www.marcprensky.com/writing/prensky%20-%20digital%20 natives,%20digital%20immigrants%20-%20part1.pdf.

Quayle, E., & Taylor, M. (2002). Child pornography and the internet: Perpetuating a cycle of abuse. *Deviant Behavior, 23,* 331–361.

Quinn, R. P. & Shepard, L. (1974). *The 1972–1973 Quality of Employment Survey.* Survey Research Center, Institute of Social Research, Ann Arbor, MI: University of Michigan Survey Research Center, Institute of Social Research.

Quinn, R. P., & Staines, G. L. (1979). *The 1977 quality of employment survey.* Ann Arbor, MI: University of Michigan Survey Research Center, Institute of Social Research.Ann Arbor: Institute for Social Research. University of Michigan.

Reese, J. T. (1986). Policing the violent society: The American experience. *Stress Medicine, 2,* 233–240.

Rege, A. (2013). Industrial Control Systems and Cybercrime. In T. J. Holt (Ed.) *Crime On-line: Causes, Correlates, and Context, 2nd edition,* (pp. 191–218). Durham, NC: Carolina Academic Press.

Reiss, A. J., Jr. (1992). Police organization in the twentieth century. In M. Tonry & N. Morris (Eds), *Modern Policing* (pp. 51–97). Chicago IL: University of Chicago Press.

Reuss-Ianni, E. (1983). *The two cultures of policing: Street cops and management cops.* New Brunswick, N. J.: Transaction Books.

Reyns, B. W., Henson, B., & Fisher, B. S. (2012). Stalking in the Twilight Zone: Extent of Cyberstalking Victimization and Offending Among College Students. *Deviant Behavior, 33,* 1–25.

Rizzo, J. R., House, R. J., & Lirtzman, S. I. (1970). Role conflict and ambiguity in complex organizations. *Administrative Science Quarterly, 15,* 150–163.

Sanders, T. (2008). *Paying for Pleasure: Men Who Buy Sex.* Cullompton: Willan Publishing.

Schell, B. H., & Dodge, J. L. (2002). *The Hacking of America: Who's Doing it, Why, and How.* Westport, CT: Quorum Books.

Schmid, A. P., & Jongman, A. J. (2005). *Political Terrorism: A New Guide to Actors, Authors, Concepts, Data Bases, Theories, & Literature.* New Brunswick, NJ: Transaction Publishers.

Senjo, S. R. (2004). An analysis of computer-related crime: Comparing police officer perceptions with empirical data. *Security Journal, 17,* 55–71.

Sharpe, K. & Earle, S. (2003). Cyberpunters and cyberwhores: Prostitution on the internet. In Y. Jewkes (Ed.), *Dot.cons. Crime, deviance and identity on the internet*, (pp. 1–14). Cullompton, UK: Willan Publishing.

Sheehan, K. B. (2001). E-mail survey response rates: A review. *Journal of Computer Mediated Communication*, 6 (2). Retrieved June 14, 2010, from http://www.ascusc.org/jcmc/vol6/issue2/sheehan.html.

Siwek, S. E. (2007). *The true cost of sound recording piracy to the U.S. economy*. Retrieved June 1, 2008, from http://www.ipi.org/ipi%5CIPIPublications.nsf/PublicationLookupFullText/5C2EE3D2107A4C228625733E0053A1F4.

Skogan, W. G. (2006). *Police and Community in Chicago: A Tale of Three Cities*. New York: Oxford University Press.

Skogan, W. G., & Hartnett, S. M. (1997). *Community policing. Chicago style*. New York: Oxford University Press.

Smith, R, Grabosky, P, & Urbas, G. (2002). *Cyber criminals on trial*. Port Melbourne: Cambridge.

Speer, D. L. (2000). Redefining borders: The challenge of cybercrime. *Crime, Law, and Social Change*, 34, 259–273.

Spielberger, C D., Westberry, L. G., Grier, K. S., & Greenfield, G. (1981). *The Police Stress Survey: Sources of Stress in Law Enforcement*. Tampa, FL: Human Resources Institute.

Stambaugh, H., Beaupre, D. S., Icove, D. J., Baker, R., Cassaday, W., & Williams, W. P. (2001). *Electronic crime needs assessment for state and local law enforcement*. Washington D.C.: National Institute of Justice. Retrieved August 3, 2010, from http://www.ncjrs.gov/pdffiles1/nij/186276.pdf.

Stevenson, J. (2007). *Welfare considerations for supervisors managing child sexual abuse on line units*. Unpublished doctoral dissertation, Middlesex University, London, UK.

Storch, J. E., & Panzarella, R. (1996). Police stress: State-trait anxiety in relation to occupational and personal stressors. *Journal of Criminal Justice*, 24, 99–107.

Symantec Corporation. (2013). *Symantec Internet security threat report, Volume 17*. Accessed June 23, 2014, from http://www.symantec.com/threatreport/.

Taylor, R.W., Fritsch, E.J., Liederbach, J., & Holt, T. J. (2010). *Digital crime and Digital Terrorism, 2nd Edition*. Upper Saddle River, NJ: PearsonPrentice Hall.

U.S. Census Bureau (2009). *Annual Estimates of the Population of Metropolitan and Micropolitan Statistical Areas: April 1, 2000 to July 1, 2008*. Retrieved July 17, 2013 from http://www.census.gov/popest/metro/tables/2008/CBSA-EST2008-01.csv.

United States Secret Service. (2014). *Electronic Crimes Task Forces and Working Groups.* Retrieved July 2, 2014 from http://www.secretservice.gov/ectf.shtml.

Van Voorhis, P., Cullen, F. T., Link, B. G., & Wolfe, N. T. (1991). The impact of race and gender on correctional officers' orientation to the integrated environment. *Journal of Research in Crime and Delinquency, 28,* 472–500.

Verini, J. (2010). The Great Cyberheist. *The New York Times.* November 14, 2010. Retrieved November 15, 2010 from http://www.nytimes.com/2010/11/14/magazine/14Hacker-t.html?_r=1.

Violanti, J. M. (1983). Stress patterns in police work: A longitudinal study. *Journal of Police Science and Administration, 11,* 211–216.

Violanti, J. M., & Aron, F. (1995). Police stressors: Variations in perception among police personnel. *Journal of Criminal Justice, 23,* 287–294.

Wall, D. S. (2001). Cybercrimes and the Internet. In D. S. Wall (Ed.), *Crime and the Internet.* (pp. 1–17). New York: Routledge.

Wall, D. S. (2004). Digital realism and the governance of spam as cybercrime. *European Journal on Criminal Policy and Research, 10,* 309–335.

Wall, D. S. 2007. *Cybercrime: The transformation of crime in the information age.* Cambridge, UK: Polity Press.

Wall, D. S., & Williams, M. (2007). Policing diversity in the digital age: Maintaining order in virtual communities. *Criminology and Criminal Justice, 7,* 391–415.

Watson, L. (2013). Al Qaeda releases guide on how to torch cars and make bombs as it names 11 public figures it wants 'dead or alive' in latest edition of its glossy magazine. *Daily Mail,* March 4, 2013. Retrieved November 12, 2013 from http://www.dailymail.co.uk/news/article-2287003/Al-Qaedareleases-guide-torch-cars-make-bombs-naming-11-public-figures-wants-dead-alivelatest-edition-glossy-magazine.html.

Weiss, D., & Marmar, C. (1997). The impact of event scale-revised. In J. Wilson and T. Keane (Eds.), *Assessing psychological trauma and PTSD* (pp. 100–110). New York: Guildford.

Wells, J. B., Minor, K. I., & Angel, E. (2009). Predictors of job stress among staff in juvenile correctional facilities. *Criminal Justice and Behavior, 36,* 245–258.

Wolak, J., Finkelhor, D., & Mitchell, K. (2012). *Trends in law enforcement responses to technology-facilitated child sexual exploitation crimes: The Third*

National Juvenile Online Victimization Study (NJOV-3). Durham, NH: Crimes against Children Research Center, 2012.

Wolfe, S. E., Higgins, G. E., & Marcum, C. D. (2008). Deterrence and digital piracy: A preliminary examination of the role of viruses. *Social Science Computer Review, 26*(3), 317–333.

Working to Halt Online Abuse. (2013). *About WHOA*. Retrieved May 20, 2014 from http://www.haltabuse.org.

Wortley, R, & Smallbone, S. (2006). *Child pornography on the Internet*. Center for Problem Oriented Policing, Guide 41. Retrieved February 2, 2011 from http://www.popcenter.org/problems/child_pornography/1.

Zhao, J., Thurman, Q., & He, N. (1999). Sources of job satisfaction among police officers: A test of demographic and work environment models. *Justice Quarterly, 16,* 153–173.

Index

Page numbers followed by "T" indicate tables; page numbers followed by "fig." indicate figures; page numbers followed by "n" indicate footnotes.

419eater.com (scam email resource), 11

A
Abdollahi, M.K. (2002), 114
Adams, R.E. (2002), 67, 69
age
    digital piracy and, 116
    job satisfaction and, 99
    job stress and, 93, 98, 103, 109
    predictors of job training and, 45–57, 46T, 47T
    seriousness of cybercrime and, 35
    stress-related alcohol consumption and, 105, 114
agency size
    cybercrime investigations and, 41–43, 42T
    job stress, satisfaction and, 98, 99
    municipal vs. rural vs. county agencies, 16–17
    overview, 58
    predictors of job training and, 46T, 47, 47T
    stress and, 91

Alarid, L.F. (2003), 70
Alpert, G.P. (2005), 28, 130
Andress, J. (2011), 4, 5, 14
Anshel, M. (1997), 90
Archbold, C.A. (2002), 91
Arcury, T.A. (2002), 67, 69
armed robbery, 31, 33
Aron, F. (1995), 98

B
Bachmann, M. (2010), 4, 7
Baker, R. (2001), 4, 5, 6, 10, 16, 17–18, 27, 28, 30, 31, 32, 36, 41, 44, 49, 59, 60, 61, 62, 66, 88, 91, 92, 93, 99, 109, 115, 123
Bayley, D. (1995), 73
Bayley, D.H. (1998), 67
Beaupre, D.S. (2001), 4, 5, 6, 10, 16, 17–18, 27, 28, 30, 31, 32, 36, 41, 44, 49, 59, 60, 61, 62, 66, 88, 91, 92, 93, 99, 109, 115, 123
Becker, W.S. (2003), 124
Belknap, J. (1992), 91, 96, 98, 103, 114
Bickart, B. (1999), 34, 45
Blevins, K.R.

(2007), 4, 8, 94, 95, 97, 99, 102, 103, 107, 109, 114, 124, 125, 127
(2010), 99, 125
(2011), 93, 94, 99, 102, 103, 107, 109, 111, 114, 124, 125
(2012), 93, 99, 124
Bocij, P. (2004), 8, 9
Bossler, A.M.
   (2009), 31, 36
   (2010), 5
   (2012), 5, 28, 29, 31, 32, 33, 59, 60, 62, 63, 64, 65, 109, 121, 123
   (2012a), 29, 30, 31, 32, 34, 35, 36, 39, 44, 123
   (2012b), 48, 49, 50, 55, 56
   (2013), 69, 70, 72, 73, 82, 83
   (2014), 28, 69, 71, 72, 73, 80, 82, 83, 87, 116
Bradshaw, R. (2008), 93, 102, 108, 109, 114, 125
Braga, A.A. (2008), 67
Brenner, S.W.
   (2008), 4, 9, 10, 11, 12, 15, 16, 22, 36, 60, 61, 66, 67, 68, 127
   (2009), 67
   (2010), 121
   (2011), 4, 12, 13
Britz, M.T.
   (2009), 91, 92
   (2010), 9
Brodsky, J. (2011), 4, 67
Bryant, C.D. (1999), 31
Bureau of Justice Assistance, 24
Bureau of Justice Statistics, 26–27
burglary, 21, 30–31, 33

Burke, R.J. (2005), 98, 103
Burkert, N. (2010), 99, 125
Burns, C.M. (2008), 93, 102, 108, 109, 114, 125
Burns, R.G. (2004), 29, 41, 61, 62, 130
businesses/high-tech industries
   cybercrime statistics involving, 26–27
   as enforcement entities, 13, 87–88, 122–23
   NIJ recommendations for, 18
   officer support for collaboration with, 72–73, 72T, 80, 82, 85T
   policy implications of research findings for, 122–23

C

Caputi, P. (1997), 90
Carson, D.C. (2013), 113
Cartwright, S. (2005), 93, 96, 99, 103, 109
Casey, E.
   (2002), 8
   (2005), 47, 91, 92
Cassaday, W. (2001), 4, 5, 6, 10, 16, 17–18, 27, 28, 30, 31, 32, 36, 41, 44, 49, 59, 60, 61, 62, 66, 88, 91, 92, 93, 99, 109, 115, 123
Catalano, S. (2012), 22, 24, 31
Center for Problem-Oriented Policing, 129
Cere, R. (2003), 10
CERTs (Computer Emergency Response Teams), 14, 66
Charlotte-Mecklenburg PD, survey of, 48–58

Chermak, S. (2006), 67
child exploitation, 8, 39, 124. See also sexual offenses, against children
child pornography
  arrests/enforcement for, 15
  Center for Problem-Oriented Policing, 129
  frequency of, 33
  officer psychological trauma from, 93, 97, 98–99, 102, 107–8, 110T–111T
  seriousness of, 27, 31, 32, 34, 36
  sexting as, 116, 121–22
Clarke, R. (2003), 7, 31, 66
Coman, G. (1991), 91, 92, 96, 99, 102, 109
community-oriented policing
  NetPolice (Finland), 129
  officer support for, survey results, 72T, 73, 74T–79T, 80, 81T, 82
  online community policing and, 69–71
  as response to cybercrime, 67–69, 127–30
computer crime units, structure of, 18, 126–30
computer crimes, 6–7
computer proficiency measures, 51, 52T, 73, 80, 81T
computer training measures, 51, 52T, 55–56, 56T
Cooper, C. (2005), 93, 96, 99, 103, 109
copyright infringement, 30–31, 33
Cordner, G.W. (1999), 67

corporations, as cybercrime victims, 8, 28–29. See also businesses/high tech industries
Corsaro, N. (2006), 67
counseling services, 19
county/sheriff offices, as law enforcement agencies, 17
Cullen, F.T.
  (1985), 90, 93, 94, 95, 96, 97, 98, 99, 102, 103, 109
  (1989), 93, 97
  (1991), 91, 95, 99
  (2007), 94, 95, 99, 102
Cunningham, S.
  (2010), 15, 27
  (2013), 8
CyberAngels group, 11–12
cyberbullying, 116–17. See also harassment, on Internet
cybercrime
  cyberterror vs., 9–10
  definitions of, 6–7
  examples of, 7–9
  frequency of, 33–34
  investigative resources for, 40–43
  primary responsibility for, 41–42
  seriousness of, 30–31, 32
  Wall's typology of, 7–9
cybercrime data/reporting. See data sources, for cybercrime; reporting of cybercrime, scope of
cybercrime exposure measures, 51, 52T
cybercrime investigation. See investigation, of cybercrime
cybercriminals, officer perceptions of, 28

cyberstalking, 12, 21, 24
cyberterror, 9–10, 32, 33–34
CyberTipline (National Center for Missing and Exploited Children), 128

D
Dale, W.M. (2003), 124
D.A.R.E. (Drug Abuse Resistance Education Program), 117
"dark figure of cybercrime," 21, 39
data sources, for cybercrime, 22–27, 117–18
  business estimates, 26–27
  IC3, 24–26, 118
  NCVS, 24, 117
  NIBRS, 23–24, 117
  UCR, 22–23
demographic measures, 51, 52T, 55, 56T
Denning, D.E. (2011), 9, 10
Dey, E.L. (1997), 34, 45
Dodge, J.L. (2002), 4, 7, 116
DOE (Department of Energy), 14
Domene, J. (2008), 93, 102, 108, 109, 114, 125
Donald, I. (2005), 93, 96, 99, 103, 109
Dowler, K. (2005), 90, 93, 97, 98
drug offenses, 30–31, 32, 33, 34
Dunham, R.G. (2005), 28, 130
Durkin, K.F.
  (1997), 8
  (1999), 31

E
education. See experience, annual training and

"Electronic Crime Scene Investigations: A Guide for First Responders" (NIJ), 16, 61
Electronic Needs Assessment for State and Local Law Enforcement (NIJ), 115. See also policy implications, for law enforcement
electronic theft, 32, 33, 34, 36
Encase software program, cost of, 91, 92
Engler, D.R. (2010), 93, 94, 97, 99, 102, 105, 107, 108, 109, 114, 124, 125, 126
Esbensen, F.A. (2013), 113
Evans, B. (1991), 91, 92, 96, 99, 102, 109
experience, annual training and
  frequency of cybercrime and, 37–38
  job satisfaction and, 102
  job stress and, 93, 98, 99
  NW3C training study, 45–48, 46T, 47T
  seriousness of cybercrime and, 35–36
extremist ideology, 9, 10

F
Facebook statistics, 3
FBI (Federal Bureau of Investigation)
  Cyber Action Teams (CATs), 120
  Infragard program, 67, 122–23
  NIBRS, 23–24
  as public policing agency, 15, 67
  UCR, 22–23

Ferraro, M. (2005), 47, 91, 92
financial crimes, enforcement of, 28, 30–31, 32, 33
Finkelhor, D.
    (2000), 8
    (2004), 23
    (2008), 4
    (2012), 3, 4, 8, 9, 40, 121, 122
    (2013), 15, 37, 116
Finn, J. (2004), 8, 9
Fisher, B.S. (2012), 21, 31
Fitzgerald, S. (2010), 5
FLETC (Federal Law Enforcement Center) survey, 32, 33–34, 63
Foltz, B.C. (2004), 10
forensic investigators, job stress and
    cost of training, 91–92
    hacking, 92
    investigation costs, 91–92
    investigative/forensic tools and, 126
    job experiences and, 93
    law enforcement administration and, 92–93
    occupational danger for, 93
    psychological trauma and, 93, 125–26
    retention, public relations, and job satisfaction, 90–91
ForensicToolKit (FTK) software program, cost of, 91
Forss, M. (2010), 67, 129
Fox, K.A. (2012), 21
Frank, J. (2007), 94, 95, 99, 102
fraud
    credit card fraud, 30–31, 33
    email-based fraud reporting, 21
    Internet fraud, 26, 29–30, 62
    in NIBRS data, 23

free speech, in United States, 9, 68
Freiburger, T.L. (2010), 5, 27, 40, 60, 130
frequency, of cybercrimes, 33–34, 37–38, 37T
Fritsch, E.J. (2010), 4, 36, 59, 61, 67

G
gender
    frequency of cybercrime, perceptions by, 37
    job stress and, 98
    predictors of job training and, 46T, 47, 47T
    seriousness of cybercrime, perceptions by, 35
    stress-related medication use and, 105
    support for workshops and, 83
Golembiewski, R.T. (1990), 92
Goodman, M.D. (1997), 4, 16, 39, 58, 60, 61, 62, 63, 99
Gormley, P.E. (2003), 98, 103, 114
governmental non-police organizations, 14–15
Grabosky, P.
    (2002), 92, 122
    (2007), 66
Graf, F.A. (1986), 91
Graves, D.C. (2007), 4, 7
G.R.E.A.T. (Gang Resistance Education and Training), 117
Greenfield, G. (1981), 92
Grier, K.S. (1981), 92
Gruen, M. (2005), 10
Gunter, W.D. (2009), 8

H

Haarr, R.
  (1999), 28, 90, 98, 103, 105, 107, 114
  (2006), 28, 90, 91, 98, 103, 109, 114
hacking, 6, 7, 28, 39, 92, 121
Hagy, D.W. (2007), 91, 99, 109
Halloran, L. (2014), 121
harassment, on Internet
  cyberbullying, 116
  cybercrime training for, 39
  frequency of, 33
  school-based programs, 116–17
  seriousness of, 30–31, 32, 34–35
Harocopos, A. (2005), 32
Hartnett, S.M. (1997), 59, 67, 68, 69, 70, 72, 73
He, N.
  (1999), 93, 98, 103, 114
  (2002), 91
Henson, B. (2012), 31
Hickman, M.J. (2006), 42
Higgins, G.E.
  (2005), 8
  (2008), 116
  (2010), 5, 27, 40, 60, 130
  (2011), 40, 44
high-tech industries. *See* businesses/high-tech industries
Hinduja, S.
  (2003), 38
  (2004), 27, 28, 31, 44, 49, 59, 62, 63, 92, 93, 109, 123, 130
  (2007), 4, 5, 16, 44, 60, 66, 88
  (2009), 3, 8
  (2012), 116
Hoffman, B. (2006), 9
Holmes, S.T. (2007), 94, 95, 99, 102
Holt, T.J.
  (2003), 14, 21, 59, 66
  (2007), 4, 7, 8, 68, 94, 97, 99, 102, 103, 107, 109, 114, 124, 125, 127
  (2009), 31, 36
  (2010), 4, 5, 36, 59, 61, 67, 99, 125
  (2011), 93, 94, 99, 102, 103, 107, 109, 111, 114, 124, 125
  (2012), 5, 10, 28, 29, 31, 32, 33, 59, 60, 62, 63, 64, 65, 93, 99, 109, 121, 123, 124
  (2012a), 29, 30, 31, 32, 34, 35, 36, 39, 44, 123
  (2012b), 48, 49, 50, 55, 56
  (2013), 7, 69, 70, 72, 73, 82, 83, 116
  (2014), 28, 69, 71, 72, 73, 80, 82, 83, 87, 116
Hough, M. (2005), 32
House, R.J. (1970), 96, 99

I

IC3 (Internet Crime Complaint Center), 24–26, 25 fig.
ICAC (Internet Crimes Against Children) task forces, 40–41, 119–20
Icove, D.J. (2001), 4, 5, 6, 10, 16, 17–18, 27, 28, 30, 31, 32, 36, 41, 44, 49, 59, 60, 61, 62, 66, 88, 91, 92, 93, 99, 109, 115, 123

identity thefts, 28, 30–31, 33
Infragard program (FBI), 67, 122–23
International Association of Chiefs of Police, 67
Internet crimes. See also community-oriented policing
  fusion centers, 120
  ISPs as enforcement entities, 12–13
  prostitution (online), 127
  reporting trends of, 25–26, 25 fig.
  seriousness of, 29–30
  task force models, 119–20
  technology and deviant activities, 3–4
  tip service (online), 128, 129
  user reporting issues, 4, 61–62, 115–16
  users, statistics, 3
  users as enforcement entities, 11–12, 66, 127–29
investigation, of cybercrime, 11–19, 19
  by businesses/high tech industries, 13, 18, 26–27, 87–88, 122–23
  costs of, 91–92
  by governmental non-police organizations, 14–15
  by Internet users, 11–12, 66, 127–29
  by ISPs, 12–13, 66, 87–88, 123
  by law enforcement (local), 17–18, 40–43, 62–63, 115–31
  by NGOs, 14
  onsite management assistance for, 18, 119–20
  overview, 89–90, 109, 114
  policy implications of research findings for, 119–20, 126–30
  priority of, 92
  by public policing agencies, 5, 15–17, 67, 119–20
  reduction/prevention strategies, 60–63, 66–71
  resources, 40–43
  responsibility for responding, 62
  stress in, 90–91
  value of, survey measures, 54
ISPs (Internet Service Providers)
  as enforcement entities, 12–13, 66, 87–88, 123
  officer support for collaboration with, 72–73, 72T, 83

J
Jenkins, P. (2001), 8
Johnson, S. (2005), 93, 96, 99, 103, 109
Jones, B.R. (2007), 67
Jones, J. (2010), 93, 94, 97, 99, 102, 105, 107, 108, 109, 114, 124, 125, 126
Jones, L.M.
  (2012), 3, 121, 122
  (2013), 15, 24, 37, 116
Jongman, A.J. (2005), 9

K
Kendall, T.
  (2010), 15, 27
  (2013), 8

Kim, B. (1990), 92
King, A. (2009), 4, 11, 21
Kohan, A. (2003), 103, 105, 114
Krause, M. (2009), 93, 102, 108, 109, 114
Krimmel, J.T. (2003), 98, 103, 114
Kwak, D. (2006), 28, 90, 91, 98, 103, 109, 114

L

Lane, F.S. (2000), 8
Langton, L. (2011), 24
law enforcement (local)
    future trends in, 20
    investigative resources for, 40–43
    NIJ recommendations for, 17–18
    policy implications of research findings for, 115–31
    responsibility for cybercrime, 62–63
law enforcement management
    LEMAS data, 19, 41–43, 42T
    NIJ recommendations for, 18
    in officer attitude survey, 62, 64
    police administrators, 30, 31, 83, 87
    policy implications of research findings for, 119–20, 124–26
    stress on officers from, 92–93
legislation, recommendations for, 18, 120–22
LEMAS (Law Enforcement Management and Administrative Statistics) data, 19, 41–43, 42T
Lemming, T. (1985), 90, 93, 94, 95, 96, 97, 98, 99, 102, 103, 109

Lenhart, A. (2007), 3, 11
Levy, S. (1984), 68
Liederbach, J. (2010), 4, 36, 59, 61, 67
Lim, V.K. (1998), 103
Link, B.G.
    (1985), 90, 93, 94, 95, 96, 97, 98, 99, 102, 103, 109
    (1989), 93, 97
    (1991), 91, 95, 99
Lirtzman, S.I. (1970), 96, 99
Lord, V.B. (1996), 28, 130
Lucas, W.L. (2003), 70
Lurigio, A.J. (1994), 70
Lutze, F. (1989), 93, 97

M

Macdonald, J.M. (2005), 28, 130
Madden, M. (2007), 3, 11
malicious software infection, 7, 30–31, 32, 34, 36, 116
Marcum, C.
    (2010), 5, 27, 40, 60, 130
    (2011), 40, 44
Marcum, C.D. (2008), 116
Marmar, C. (1997), 108
Martelli, J. (1989), 92
Martelli, T. A. (1989), 92
Martin, G. (2006), 9
Mastrofski, S.D. (1995), 67
Mazmanian, D. (2003), 103, 105, 114
McGarrell, E.F. (2006), 67
McGrath, M.G. (2002), 8
McQuade, S. (2006), 4, 16, 60, 62, 66
media piracy (unauthorized copying), 32, 33–34, 35, 37, 116
mental health resources, 19

use of, 106T, 108–9, 114,
   125–26
 use of counseling, 112T–113T,
   114
Mikkelsen, A. (2005), 98, 103
Miller, S. (1999), 67, 69, 70
Millet, C. (2005), 93, 96, 99, 103,
   109
Milrod, C. (2012), 8
Mitchell, K.
   (2012), 4, 8, 9, 40, 121
   (2013), 15, 37, 116
Mitchell, K.J.
   (2000), 8
   (2012), 3, 121, 122
   (2013), 24
Mizota, K. (2013), 91
Morash, M.
   (1999), 28, 90, 98, 103, 105,
     107, 114
   (2006), 28, 90, 91, 98, 103,
     109, 114
Morley, J. (2008), 93, 102, 108,
   109, 114, 125
municipal law enforcement agencies, 16
Myers, S.M. (2000), 70

N

National Center for Missing and
   Exploited Children, 128
Nazario, J. (2003), 4
NCVS (National Crime Victimization Survey), 24, 117
NetPolice (Finland), 129
Newman, G. (2003), 7, 31, 66
NGOs (non-governmental organizations), 14
Nhan, J. (2013), 12

NIBRS (National Incident Based
   Reporting System), 23–24, 117
NIJ (National Institute of Justice)
   cyberterror, definition, 10
   "Electronic Crime Scene Investigations: A Guide for First
     Responders" (NIJ), 16, 61
   Electronic Needs Assessment
     for State and Local Law Enforcement (NIJ), 115
   report, policy implications for
     local law enforcement,
     115–30
   report, recommendations for
     local law enforcement,
     17–18, 41, 61
   training manual, 16
Nobles, M.R. (2012), 21
Novak, K.J. (2003), 70
NSA (National Security Agency), 15
NW3C (National White Collar
   Crime Center), 24
   officer perceptions of cybercrime, assessment by,
     34–38, 36T
   survey, on officer cybercrime
     training, 45–48
   training by, 44–45, 119

O

officer perceptions, of cybercrime,
   19, 27–38
   assessing perceptions, 34–38,
     36T, 37T, 39
   of cybercriminals and victims,
     28–29
   as first responders, 16, 19, 44,
     60–63, 107–9

of frequency, 33–34, 37–38, 37T
and Internet, survey measures, 51–53, 52T–53T, 57–58, 57T
by patrol officers, 28
and policing, survey measures, 53–54, 57T, 58
prioritization, by law enforcement, 27–28
of seriousness, 29–32, 34–36, 36T
of uniqueness, 29
officer perceptions, of responses to cybercrime, 19, 59–88
of importance within police departments, 63–66
overview, 59, 88
of traditional strategies, 60–63
online harassment, 8–9, 31, 32
ordered logistic regression models, online community policing survey, 82–83, 84T, 86T
Ornod, R. (2004), 23
Osgood, D.W. (2013), 113

P

Panzarella, R. (1996), 98
Paoline, E.A. (2000), 70
Patchin, J.W.
 (2009), 3, 8
 (2012), 116
Patterson, G.T. (2003), 98, 114
pedophilia, on Internet, 30, 31, 33. See also sexual offenses, against children
Pelfrey, W.V. (2004), 69, 73
Peretti, K.K. (2009), 7, 92, 122

Perez, L.M. (2010), 93, 94, 97, 99, 102, 105, 107, 108, 109, 114, 124, 125, 126
PERF (Police Executive Research Forum) study, 43
Peterson, D. (2013), 113
Petrone, S. (1985), 109
Picarelli, J. (2012), 124
piracy (unauthorized copying), 32, 33–34, 35, 37, 116
police administrators, 30, 31, 83, 87
policy implications, for law enforcement, 115–31
for business/high-tech industry, 122–23
for computer crime units, 126–30
for data reporting, 117–18
for electronic crime units/task forces, 119–20
for investigative/forensic tools, 126
for legislation, 120–22
for management, 124–26
for public awareness, 115–17
for research, 123–24
for training/certification courses, 118–19
Pollitt, M.M. (1998), 10
Prensky, M. (2001), 3
property offenses, seriousness of, 31
prostitution (online), 127
public awareness
importance of, 61
NIJ recommendation for, 17
online community policing and, 70–71

policy implications of research findings for, 115–17, 118
public policing agencies, 5, 15–17, 67, 119–20

Q
Quayle, E. (2002), 8
Quinn, R.P. (1974), 95

R
race
    frequency of cybercrime and, 37–38
    job stress and, 98
    predictors of job training and, 46T, 47, 47T
    seriousness of cybercrime and, 35
Radvanovsky, R. (2011), 4, 67
Reaves, B.A. (2006), 42
Rege, A. (2013), 4, 67
Reiser, M. (1985), 109
reporting of cybercrime, scope of. See also officer perceptions, of cybercrime
    by businesses, 4, 27
    data sources, 22–27, 117–18
    NIJ recommendation for, 18
    overview, 19, 21–22, 38, 39
research, on cybercrime. See also surveys/studies
    NIJ recommendations, 18
    policy implications for, 123–24, 130
    recommendations for, 118, 119, 122, 123–24, 126, 129–30
Reuss-Ianni, E. (1983), 69
Reyns, B.W. (2012), 21, 31
Ricketts, M.L. (2010), 5, 27, 40, 60, 130
Rizzo, J.R. (1970), 96, 99
Robertson, M. (1997), 90
Rohe, W.M. (2002), 67, 69

S
Sachau, D. (2010), 93, 94, 97, 99, 102, 105, 107, 108, 109, 114, 124, 125, 126
Sanders, T. (2008), 4
satisfaction, in policing. See also stress, in policing
    assessment of stress and, 94–98, 124–25
    correlation matrix for, 99, 101T
    effects of stress on retention, public relations, and, 90–91
    forensic investigators, job stress and, 90–91
    job experience and, 99
    predictors of stress and, 98–103, 100T, 101T, 102T
    regression model for, 99, 102T, 109
    research, dependent variables on, 95–96
Savannah-Chatham Metropolitan PD, survey of, 48–58
scams, on Internet, 26
Schell, B. (2002), 4, 7, 116
Schmid, A.P. (2005), 9
Schmittlein, D. (1999), 34, 45
Secret Service (U.S.), 15
Senjo, S.R. (2004), 5, 28, 29, 30, 31, 38, 39, 41, 46, 49, 92, 93, 99, 109, 130
seriousness, of cybercrimes

assessment of law enforcement management and, 64
officer perceptions, 29–32
officer perceptions, assessment of, 34–36, 36T
sexting, as child pornography, 116, 121–22
sexual offenses, against children. See also child pornography
child exploitation, 8, 39, 124
CyberTipline, 128
investigative resources, 40–41
in NIBRS data, 23–24
pedophilia, 30, 31, 33
sexting as, 116, 121–22
watchdog groups, 11–12
Shearing, C. (1995), 73
Sheehan, K.B. (2001), 34, 45
Shelly, J.K. (1992), 91, 96, 98, 103, 114
Shepard, L. (1974), 95
shoplifting, 30–31, 33
Siwek, S.E. (2007), 8
Skogan, W.G.
(1994), 70
(1997), 59, 67, 68, 69, 70, 72, 73
(2006), 67, 73
Smallbone, S. (2006), 129
Smith, R. (2002), 92, 122
Snipes, J.B. (1995), 67
social media, 11–12, 127–28
software piracy. See piracy (unauthorized copying)
spam emails, data collection of, 117
Speilberger, C.D. (1981), 92
Stambaugh, H. (2001), 4, 5, 6, 10, 16, 17–18, 27, 28, 30, 31, 32, 36, 41, 44, 49, 59, 60, 61, 62, 66, 88, 91, 92, 93, 99, 109, 115, 123
state police agencies, 17
statistics
on arrests for child exploitation crimes, 8, 40–41
correlation, definition, 46 n.1
on cybercrime training, 44
on cyberstalking, 24
data sources, 22–27, 117–18
on Facebook user accounts, 3
hierarchical ordinary least squares regression, 54–56, 56T
on Internet crime reporting trends, 25–26, 25 fig.
on Internet users, 3
on law enforcement agency sizes, 16
losses from cybercrime, 7
NIJ recommendations, 18
on online community policing, 73, 74T–79T, 80
on predictors of job training, 46T, 47T
regression, definition, 46–47
on seriousness of cybercrime, 34–36, 36T
on unsolved burglaries, 21
Stevenson, J. (2007), 93, 94, 102, 107, 108, 109
Storch, J.E. (1996), 98
stress, in policing, 90–105. See also satisfaction, in policing
administration and, 92–93
coping mechanisms for, 103–5, 104T, 114
cybercrime forensic investigation costs and, 91–92

digital evidence handling experience and, 97
hacking, investigation/prosecution and, 92
job dangerousness and, 97
job experiences and, 93
occupational danger and, 93
predictors of satisfaction and, 98–103, 100T, 101T, 102T
psychological trauma and, 93, 105–9, 106T, 110T–111T, 125–26
research, correlation matrix for, 98–99, 100T
research, dependent variables, 94–95, 95T
research, work-related variables, 96–97
retention/satisfaction and, 90–91
role conflict and, 96, 98
street crime, 89
supervisory support and, 96–97
Sundt, J.L. (2007), 94, 95, 99, 102
surveys/studies
on agency responsibility, 41–43, 42T
business victimization survey, 26–27
on coping mechanisms, 103–5, 104T
on cybercrime frequency, 33–34, 37–38, 37T
on cybercrime seriousness, 29–31, 32, 34–36, 36T
on cybercrime training, 45–58, 46T, 47T, 50T, 52T–53T, 56T–57T, 63–64
on cybercrime uniqueness, 29
NCVS-Supplemental Survey, 24, 117
on online child exploitation crimes, 40–41
on psychological trauma, 105–9, 106T
on responses to Internet fraud, 62
on strategies to improve response, 60–63, 66–71
on stress and job satisfaction, 93, 94–98, 107–9, 110T–111T, 112T–113T
on stress and job satisfaction predictors, 99–103, 100T–102T, 109–14, 110T–111T, 112T–113T
on support for cybercrime investigations, 63–66
on support/predictors increasing support, for online community policing, 69–71, 72–88, 72T, 74T–79T, 81T, 84T–86T
on technological needs of police, 43

T

Target, as cybercrime victim, 8
task forces, 40–41, 119–20. See also computer crime units, structure of
Taylor, M. (2002), 8
Taylor, P. (2005), 93, 96, 99, 103, 109
Taylor, R.W. (2010), 4, 36, 59, 61, 67
Taylor, T.J. (2013), 113

Teo, T.S. (1998), 103
terrorist attacks, 9, 32
terrorist attacks against electronic targets, 33
Thomas, J. (2009), 4, 11, 21
Thompson, C.Y. (2004), 29, 41, 61, 62, 130
Thurman, Q. (1999), 93, 98, 103, 114
training, attitudes towards, 19, 48–58
  overview, 39, 58
  survey demographics and descriptive statistics, 50–54, 52T–53T, 73, 74T–79T, 80
  survey factors associated with interest in, 48–49
  survey results, 49–58
  survey results, officer interest, 50T
training/certification courses, 43–48
  ICAC program training, 40
  limiting factors, 44
  NIJ recommendation, 18, 41
  NW3C training study, 45–48, 46T, 47T
  by police academies, 44–45
  policy implications of research findings for, 118–19
  real vs. virtual crimes and, 29
  statistics, of cybercrime training, 44

U

UCR (Uniform Crime Report), 22–23, 117
uniqueness, of cybercrimes, 29
Urbas, G. (2002), 92, 122

V

Van Voorhis, P. (1991), 91, 95, 99
vandalism, 30–31, 32, 33
Verini, J. (2010), 8
victims, of cybercrime
  avoidance of victimization, 127–28
  IC3, as data source on, 24–26
  NCVS, as data source on, 24
  officer perceptions of, 28–29
  officers as first responders, 16
  underreporting of cybercrime by, 21
Violanti, J. M.
  (1983), 98, 114
  (1995), 98
viruses (computer), 33

W

Wall, D.S.
  (2001), 4, 7–9, 22, 31, 33, 59, 61, 66, 67, 68, 71, 127
  (2004), 4
  (2007), 7, 11, 12, 14, 15, 16, 47, 59, 60, 66, 67, 68, 92
Waters, L.K. (1989), 92
Watson, L. (2013), 10
website, for scam email reporting, 11
Weiss, D. (1997), 108
Weitzer, R. (2012), 8, 127
Westberry, L.G. (1981), 92
Whitworth, K.H. (2004), 29, 41, 61, 62, 130
Williams, M. (2007), 66, 67, 68
Williams, W.P. (2001), 4, 5, 6, 10, 16, 17–18, 27, 28, 30, 31, 32, 36, 41, 44, 49, 59, 60, 61, 62,

66, 88, 91, 92, 93, 99, 109, 115, 123
Wilson, J.M. (2006), 67
Winterfeld, S. (2011), 4, 5, 14
Wolak, J.
   (2000), 8
   (2012), 4, 8, 9, 40, 121
   (2013), 15, 37, 116
Wolfe, N.T.
   (1989), 93, 97
   (1991), 91, 95, 99
Wolfe, S.E. (2008), 116
Worden, R.E.
   (1995), 67
   (2000), 70
Working to Halt Online Abuse (WHOA), 12
workshops, on cybercrime, 68–69, 83
Wortley, R. (2006), 129
Wozniak, J.F. (1985), 90, 93, 94, 95, 96, 97, 98, 99, 102, 103, 109

Z

Zhao, J.
   (1999), 93, 98, 103, 114
   (2002), 91